$$1+1=1$$

1 + 1 = 1

Creating a Multiracial Church
from Single Race Congregations

Derek Chinn

☙PICKWICK *Publications* · Eugene, Oregon

1 + 1 = 1
Creating a Multiracial Church from Single Race Congregations

Copyright © 2012 Derek Chinn. All rights reserved. Except for brief quotations in critical publications or reviews, no part of this book may be reproduced in any manner without prior written permission from the publisher. Write: Permissions, Wipf and Stock Publishers, 199 W. 8th Ave., Suite 3, Eugene, OR 97401.

Pickwick Publications
An Imprint of Wipf and Stock Publishers
199 W. 8th Ave., Suite 3
Eugene, OR 97401

www.wipfandstock.com

ISBN 13: 978-1-62032-238-3

ESV Copyright and Permissions Information
The Holy Bible, English Standard Version® (ESV®)
Copyright © 2001 by Crossway, a publishing ministry of Good News Publishers.
All rights reserved.
ESV Text Edition: 2007

Scripture quotations marked (NLT) are taken from the Holy Bible, New Living Translation, copyright © 1996, 2004, 2007 by Tyndale House Foundation. Used by permission of Tyndale House Publishers, Inc., Carol Stream, Illinois 60188. All rights reserved.

Scripture notations marked (NIV) are taken from the Holy Bible, New International Version®, NIV®. Copyright © 1973, 1978, 1984, 2011 by Biblica, Inc.™ Used by permission of Zondervan. All rights reserved worldwide. www.zondervan.com.

The "NIV" and "New International Version" are trademarks registered in the United States Patent and Trademark Office by Biblica, Inc.™

EMERSON, MICHAEL O.; PEOPLE OF THE DREAM. © 2006 by Princeton University Press. Reprinted by permission of Princeton University Press.

OUP Material: CROSSING THE ETHNIC DIVIDE by Kathleen Garces-Foley (2007) Table 4.1 from p. 95 (adapted). By permission of Oxford University Press, Inc.

Cataloging-in-Publication data:

Chinn, Derek.

   1 + 1 = 1 : creating a multiracial church from single race congregations / Derek Chinn.

   x + 134 p. ; 23 cm. Includes bibliographical references and index.

   ISBN 13: 978-1-62032-238-3

   1. Race relations—Religious aspects—Christianity. 2. Multiculturalism—Religious aspects—Christianity. 3. Ethnicity—Religious aspects—Christianity. 4. Church work with minorities—United States. I. Title.

BT734.2 C277 2012

Manufactured in the U.S.A.

For Jean,
with love and gratitude

Contents

List of Figures viii
Foreword by Michael O. Emerson ix

1: The Need For New Math 1
2: A Challenge to the Status Quo 9
3: What Others Say and Think 19
4: Churches that Became Multiracial through Merging 44
5: A New Philosophy 67
6: Key Challenges of Forming Multiracial Congregations through Mergers 75
7: Opportunities of this Ministry Approach 111
8: Conclusion 120

Bibliography 125
Scripture Index 129
Author Index 131
Subject Index 132

Table of Figures

Figure 3.1 – Principles for a Multiracial Church 25
Figure 3.2 – Types of Multiethnic Congregations 31
Figure 4.1 – Churches Studied by Parent Congregation Characteristics 47
Figure 4.2 – Synopsis of Reasons for Bringing Congregations Together 48
Figure 6.1 – Principles for a Multiracial Church by Corresponding Attributes 90
Figure 6.2 – Impetus for Change, Diversification Source, and Multiracial Congregational Types 102
Figure 6.3 – Framework for Multiracial Merge Process 107

Foreword

by Dr. Michael Emerson

1 + 1 = 1 is not only a wonderfully titled book; it is a wonderful book. When I read Derek Chinn's work, I was ecstatic that someone had written on a topic in which we currently have so little understanding: merging congregations each filled with people of different racial backgrounds, to become one new multiracial congregation.

This is an important model, but too rarely practiced by congregations, in good part because (a) so little is known about the rewards and pitfalls of attempting mergers of congregations with people of different backgrounds, and (b) the subsequent uncertainty as to how to go about merging congregations and the consequences of doing so. Dr. Chinn's work is a gigantic step forward, filling a gaping hole in our understanding.

His work is based on the study of real congregations engaged in the real process of merging different-race congregations. So much wisdom is packed into this book that it will surely be used by many to understand the processes, steps, and events that occur when attempting to merge different-race congregations. With Dr. Chinn's permission, I have been using some of what is written in this book when I speak to denominational and other church leaders. It is essential knowledge.

The future of the church, I am convinced, rests in significant part on the movement toward Jesus' prayer for us in John 17—that we would be one, so that we may a true and complete witness to the world. How we come together in unity can vary. This book offers us an essential model, one that I hope will be considered and adapted by more churches across the globe. But the book you are about to read does more than offer a model. It provides a theological basis for doing so, and actual practices that enhance the opportunity for unity.

Foreword

This is a fascinating book, highly original, vitally important. Read it with eyes wide open, and may its wisdom be as much a blessing to you as it has been to me. All for One!

Dr. Michael Emerson
Allyn & Gladys Cline Professor of Sociology and Co-Director of Kinder Institute for Urban Research at Rice University

1

The Need For New Math

For newlyweds, Mike and Carol were fairly comfortable with the typical adjustments to married life. It was a second marriage for both so things were familiar. However, complicating this new relationship were the kids that both husband and wife brought into the marriage. He had three boys. She brought along three girls. Yet, anyone who had seen or met them all, would have thought they were idyllic for a blended family.

It is commonly understood that life in fiction is easier than the harsh truths of reality. The television show, *The Brady Bunch*, gives the impression that blending two different households together will work well as long as they are bound together by love. The same could be said of the church. What could be more wonderful than bringing congregations of different races together to create one, united multiracial body? It is theologically sound to presume that when Christ is central, two churches should be able to navigate joining together fairly well.

The problem for the church is that fiction gives way to reality. And, when reality asserts itself on the unprepared, things can go sideways with painful consequences.

> **9** *After this I looked, and behold, a great multitude that no one could number, from every nation, from all tribes and peoples and languages, standing before the throne and before the Lamb, clothed in white robes, with palm branches in their hands,* **10** *and crying out with a loud voice, "Salvation belongs to our God who sits on the throne, and to the Lamb!"* **11** *And all the angels were standing around the throne and around the elders and the four living creatures, and they fell on their faces before the throne and worshiped God,* **12** *saying, "Amen! Blessing and glory and wisdom and thanksgiving and honor*

and power and might be to our God forever and ever! Amen." (Rev 7:9–12, ESV)

Of the many, if not all, things the church will do for the love and service of Jesus, Rev 7:9–10 reveals that worshipping with the diverse Body of Christ will be a dominant feature of an eternity with him. The magnitude of who Jesus is and what he has done provokes this worship—the Apostle John recounts that the blood of Christ was shed for people from every tribe, tongue, and nation.[1]

What keeps the church from participating in this eternal chorus now?

One People Fellowship (OPF)[2] was born Easter 2006. It was birthed when Faith Bible Church (FBC), a predominantly Asian-American congregation joined with another congregation, Grace Community Church (GCC), an Anglo congregation, to form a church that intentionally sought to bring people of different racial cultures together.

The process of bringing FBC and GCC together took about two years, beginning with the two churches holding a joint event together. The event went well and prompted the leadership of both churches to hold a few more ministry events together. The success of these subsequent events led the core leaders of both churches to dream about what they might accomplish as one congregation.

After substantial prayer and dialogue, the leaders believed that combining the two churches was God's desire. A vision for what the new church would look like and how it would operate was presented by the elders of each congregation to their people. Core leadership from each church worked together to develop a plan for making the unification happen.

Joining the two churches together was not an easy task. At one point, the plan to unite was abandoned. Caught by surprise about the turn of events, the elders of the two churches scrutinized the difficulties leading to the decision to stop the process. The reasons were found to be insufficient, and the effort to join together was revived with new vigor. The churches met together as one congregation for the first time on Easter Day, 2006.

---

1. Rev 5:9–14
2. All churches and people are represented by pseudonyms.

Challenge and Opportunity for Our Day

The racial makeup of the population in the United States is changing. With regard to racial diversity, Gerardo Marti points out, "The United States continues to become more diverse in every societal sphere, bringing a new challenge to integration to both civic and religious organizations. Demographers estimate that by the year 2050, America will have no single majority group."[3]

More recent projections by the U.S. government indicate that by 2042, the minority population will overtake the majority Anglo population.[4] As the population shifts, the church faces a unique challenge and opportunity to explore if and how it will minister across cultures.

Racial integration in the church has often been ignored by leaders and laity because of a preference for segregation within the Body of Christ.[5] The status quo favors segregation as Michael O. Emerson and Christian Smith observe,

> In a pluralistic market, and given that most people seek the greatest gain for the least cost, internally diverse congregations are typically at a disadvantage. The key generalization is this: the cost of producing meaning, belonging, and security in *internally diverse* congregations is usually much greater—because of the increased complexity of demands, needs, and backgrounds, the increased effort necessary to create social solidarity and group identity, and the greater potential for internal conflict. Thus, *internally homogeneous congregations more often provide what draws people to religious groups for a lower cost than do internally diverse congregations.*[6]

In other words, racial integration in a church is more costly than segregation. Yet, the church's self-imposed racial segregation will be less tenable as society's various institutions (e.g., schools, business, non-religious social organizations) become more integrated reflecting the changes occurring in the general population.

---

3. Marti, *Mosaic*, 22.
4. Ohlemacher, "White Americans," line 1.
5. Luo, "Asian-American," lines 17–19.
6. Emerson and Smith, *Divided*, 145.

Factors such as age[7] and mortality[8] contribute to the demographic changes the U.S. is experiencing—people are living longer. For some churches, the average age of members is rising and a lack of younger congregants is leading to the gradual passing of these congregations.[9]

The suburban area where OPF is located has a changing racial population that mirrors that of the country. According to U.S. census bureau 2011 estimates,[10] Washington County (near Portland, Oregon) has an Anglo, non-Hispanic population that is 69 percent of the total population. These same census estimates indicate that within the total population, the Hispanic/Latino community represents 16 percent, Asians are about 9 percent, Blacks are 2 percent, and people identifying with two or more races are at a little under 4 percent.

The population OPF serves will continue to become more racially and ethnically diverse. For the county, current population estimates indicate that the minority population is roughly 30 percent, and will only increase as the overall population grows.

According to a local parachurch ministry that maintains a database of churches in the Portland metro region,[11] there are over 270 culturally-oriented/ethnic-specific congregations[12] in the area (out of approximately 1,200, as of April 2009).[13] There are only about 30 churches/ministries that consider themselves multi-ethnic.

As the racial demographics continue to change across the country,[14] how will the church respond to this flux?

A traditional strategy would advocate increasing the number of racial-specific ministries. Various approaches to minister to distinct racial groups include planting new churches, making existing churches more welcoming to racial minorities, partnering with ethnic-focused congregations, and encouraging majority churches to host ethnic congregations within their

---

7. Tanneberg, "An Aging Society."
8. Smietana, "Southern Baptists," lines 12–13.
9. Hadaway, *FACTs*, 3.
10. U.S. Census Bureau, "Washington County, Oregon."
11. Mission Portland (missionportland.org)
12. While predominantly non-white congregations, some are immigrant congregations ministering to Eastern Europeans.
13. missionportland.org/churches.
14. Roberts, "Minorities," lines 1–7.

facility. Notably, most of these tactics maintain segregation between people groups along racial and ethnic lines.

It has been observed that churches not only unite around doctrines and beliefs, but also social similarities—people wanting to be with those who are like them.[15] This sociological observation, also referred to as the Homogeneous Unit Principle (HUP), reflects and influences how ministry is done by the church. In his critique of the HUP, Bruce Fong describes such an affinity in this way, "A typical city population in the U.S.A. is comprised of people with varying economic, education, and cultural ties. The HUP theory acknowledges these social dynamics and works with them in an effort to attract as many as possible to Christ."[16] This social affinity values minimizing conflict across social constructs in order to maximize receptivity to the gospel.

Inhibiting conflict for the gospel's sake can be an admirable goal, but there are compelling reasons to consider engaging conflict on behalf of the gospel. Healthy and fruitful conflict engagement is a necessary part of integrating racial groups intentionally.

While the "church growth" principle of affinity along racial and ethnic lines is one manner of how the kingdom of God grows, this study focuses on another avenue—establishing a multiracial church. Sociologists have observed the same opportunity: "As the number of interracial families in America continues to increase, and as the diversity of certain metropolitan areas increases, interracial religious organizations will likely have a greater degree of fitness in those environments."[17]

An Alternative Option for These Opportunities

Given the demographic changes taking place—a growing racial minority population and aging congregations leading to church closures—there is an opportunity for the church. Multiracial congregations can be created by merging single race churches together.

Bringing congregations together to create one multiracial church community is not without significant challenges. The challenges include moving against the human tendency to associate with those most like

---

15. McGavran, *Church Growth*, 223–27.
16. Fong, *Racial Equality*, 37.
17. Christerson et al., *Against*, 166.

oneself, bridging racial/ethnic differences and expectations, resolving conflict in a healthy manner, and leading with intention, clarity, and sensitivity.

This work examines two aspects of creating a multiracial church when two congregations join together. First, it will consider the theological basis for bringing separate and racially distinct churches together. Second, it will explore the practical application of this theology. This will be accomplished by investigating the experiences of six churches in the Pacific Northwest taking this particular ministry approach.

Utilizing surveys, interviews, and secondary research, this book reveals the challenges of bringing congregations together to create a multiracial church. The case will be made for why a multiracial church is a plausible starting point for churches looking to merge with others, identify factors that contribute to "success" when merging single race churches, clarify the unique obstacles single race congregations will face when becoming multiracial, and discuss the dynamics of these obstacles.

Getting on the Same Page with Terms

Diversity can mean a number of things to different people. For the sake of this text, defining terms will facilitate discussion on the subject. Following are terms used throughout the book and how this author understands these words and concepts.

- *Race*—"a culturally determined classification of people derived from accepted (and often stereotyped) ways of observing and evaluating heritable physical characteristics."[18] Race is a category based on alleged genetic differences (i.e., Black, White, Hispanic, Native American/First Nations, and Asian).

- *Ethnicity*—"a culturally or socially constructed category based on presumed social or cultural differences."[19] Therefore, Chinese is distinct from Japanese or Korean, even though they are associated with the same racial group, Asian. Likewise, people of European descent as Italian, Czech, Scottish, or Finn are collectively of the Anglo or white race.

- *Multicultural*—composed of different cultures, where culture represents beliefs, behaviors, values, interests, and traits expressed in

18. Angrosino, *Talking*, 10.
19. Ibid., 12.

conduct and thought. This represents the broadest range and most vague of the "multi-" definitions. Culture can be segmented along age, gender, hobbies, personal preferences, size, race, ethnicity, and a host of other criteria. It is frequently used to indicate diversity of ethnicity and race.

- *Multiethnic*—different ethnic backgrounds or heritages are present and distinguished apart from race.
- *Multiracial*—different racial groups are represented, where no single racial group comprises more than 80 percent of the population.[20] Because "multiracial" has a specific, measurable distinction and takes into account the nature of a racialized society, it will be the preferred definition of this work. However, in this book's citations, deference to the terms the authors and sources use will be given—original use and intent of words to describe diversity will be respected and maintained.
- *Racialization*—the concept that race affects one's life to the extent that it impacts their life experiences. Race determines how a person interacts and is perceived within the social environment. More specifically stated, "a racialized society is a society where race matters profoundly for differences in life experiences, life opportunities, and social relationships."[21]
- *Single race congregation*—a church with one race representing more than 80 percent of the congregation's racial make-up.
- *Ethnic transcendence*—a ministry strategy that supersedes ethnic identity. It moves people to adopt a new identity shaped by new interests and exchanges a preference for ethnic identity for an overriding identity.[22]
- *Intercultural*—cultural integration where there are people of different ethnic and racial cultures interacting with one another, not just composition.[23]
- *Church merger*—joining together two or more distinct church congregations to form one congregation. In the process, both churches unite their people and assets to form a new identity and organization.

20. Yancey, *One Body*, 15.
21. Emerson and Smith, *Divided*, 7.
22. Marti, *Mosaic*, 172–79.
23. Baker, " Intercultural Notes," 3.

Why Would You Spend Your Hard Earned Shekels on This Book?

If you are part of a church interested in becoming a multiracial/cross-cultural ministry by joining single-race congregations together, this is for you! These churches include congregations that are "dying" or "plateauing," facing demographic change in their existing geographic location, and/or have a crisis of resource(s) that can be offset by another congregation. Urban ministry would be an appropriate application of this approach. As communities and neighborhoods change, churches can transition without being "lost" to the demographic shift. Joining congregations together is good stewardship of the resources God has given to his people.

Contrary to accepted wisdom, this ministry approach is not limited to churches with "no options left." This work is profitable to ministries seeking a proactive way to engage their local community. Churches considering merging will find this book offers a distinct dimension not found in existing resources.

This book also contributes to the conversation concerning multiracial church planting/start-ups. Bringing congregations together to form one church offers a biblically consistent perspective on reconciliation, conflict resolution and, where race and ethnicity are concerned, cross-cultural relationships.

Churches or ministries that want to extend their racial or cultural reach can benefit by considering an option they may not have been aware of or deemed unworkable. Regardless of motivation (e.g., survival, evangelism, passing along assets to a younger generation of believers, or to remove perceived barriers to inclusion), this endeavor offers an avenue of doing ministry that may have been overlooked or prematurely dismissed.

This work started as the author's dissertation and is, at heart, an academic product. However, revisions have been made to reduce its somnolent qualities. Kidding aside, thank you for reading this book. I hope it will encourage the church and move God's people to expand the kingdom by modeling Christ's redemptive work in a unique, challenging way.

2

A Challenge to the Status Quo

AN OLD ADAGE SAYS, "If it ain't broke, don't fix it." In other words, if the status quo works, why mess with it? A retort to said adage responds, "Who says it ain't broke?"

The multiracial church offers both a daunting challenge and an enticing promise to the church. God invites his people to a change that appears unfamiliar to most. A multiracial church seems to go against conventional wisdom for how the gospel is presented and faith is practiced in the United States.

No one dismisses the notion that the Body of Christ is comprised of various races and ethnicities. They may even affirm that this is how the local Body should look. Yet in practice, few explore the potential of this congregational composition. Emerson estimates that "7 percent of American congregations are multiracial."[1]

Church mergers are not typically seen as a proactive ministry strategy. Rather, it is perceived as an action of last resort. Richard Laribee sums up the negative perception associated with church mergers, "Unfortunately, congregations seldom merge in order to add value to their ministries. More often, congregational mergers are sought as a means to continue offering pre-existing programs that no longer attract people, bolster declining budgets, fill empty pews, or postpone the closure of dwindling congregations that no longer attract the community."[2] Put succinctly, churches only

---

1. Emerson and Woo, *People*, 36. In a 2010 presentation given at the Multiethnic church Conference in San Diego, CA, Dr. Emerson reports that this percentage has not changed from 1998 when the study was conducted and 2007 when follow-up occurred.

2. Laribee, *Factors*, 117.

consider merging if they are in trouble—it is a last ditch effort to stay alive . . . without having to change.[3]

Besides a headache, what could be gained by doing ministry in a way that leads to conflict and is viewed as an act of desperation? How would tackling two difficult tasks advance the kingdom of God when settling one issue is sufficiently challenging?

Framing things in a different light, "What does God do to move people from Gen 11, the Tower of Babel, to Rev 5, the Throne of God?" How does God take people who are scattered throughout the world, separated by language and race, and bring them together for eternity as one people? Bringing two congregations together to create a multiracial ministry offers a picture of this renewal and future eternal reality.

Borrowing from the popular campaign slogan of U.S. President Barack Obama, God invites us, His people, the church, to participate in change we can believe in.

One day, one of our congregants was visiting with us at our home. I asked our guest her thoughts about the plan to combine our Asian congregation with another congregation (Anglo). As a regular attendee, I expected her answer to be as positive as others had been. I was surprised when she expressed hope that it would not happen. Invited to expand on her answer, she commented that she had been part of a church merge in the past, and it did not go well. Then, she described the unfortunate circumstances that affected her and her family after the churches came together.

Since that conversation, I have wondered about what could have been said and done to reassure this person that the direction Faith Bible Church was heading did not have to end the way she expected. In subsequent months, there were a couple more families that did not continue on with the new church. Was there something the leadership missed or failed to do to allay fears?

The author proposes that there are three main elements to think through when forming multiracial congregations from single-race church communities: 1) what comprises and cultivates a multiracial ministry? 2) how does one engage the change and conflict that will occur?[4] and 3) what is the plan for "merging" congregations together?

---

3. In the case of multisite mergers, typically one church is ailing. A longer discussion on these mergers is found in chapter 3.

4. The rationale for discussing change is that it is a common denominator for both creating a multiracial ministry and forming a new church from two congregations.

These elements will be examined within the structure of three perspectives –theological, written research, and the experience of churches that took this ministry approach—bringing congregations together to create a multiracial church environment.

A Theological Perspective

The Multiracial Church Is Normative

Now there were in the church at Antioch prophets and teachers, Barnabas, Simeon who was called Niger, Lucius of Cyrene, Manaen a member of the court of Herod the tetrarch, and Saul. (Acts 13:1, ESV)

Acts 11 and 13 describe a church that has a demographic cutting across a wide spectrum. Looking at some of the leaders of the church in Acts 13:1, we find a Jew from Cyprus (Barnabas), two Gentiles from Africa (Simeon and Lucius), a Gentile educated in Rome (Manaen), and a Jew (Saul) from Tarsus, all in the Roman province of Cilicia (modern-day Turkey). Besides having a diverse leadership, the church in Antioch, Syria, served a diverse community because it was established in a thriving international trade center.[5]

Acts 15 reports that this diversity caused concern for other believers, particularly those of Jewish descent. Church leadership took up the issue when a dispute arose concerning the lifestyle practices of the Gentiles. The leaders mediated a solution for the disagreement and affirmed the kinship of Jew and Gentile in Christ.

The Apostle Paul, well-acquainted with the church in Antioch, reveals God's heart in Eph 2—Jesus, by his crucifixion, has broken down the wall that previously divided Jew from non-Jew/Gentile. Furthermore, not only are Jews and Gentiles no longer separated, but they are unified—Jesus united these two people groups.[6] "The peace that Christ brought must result in a new man that challenges previous schemes of 'insiders' and 'outsiders' and lives in mutual acceptance of each other. A history of selectivity is replaced by oneness in Christ and a new history of brotherhood of inclusiveness is displayed."[7]

---

5. CTSP. "Syrian."
6. Eph 2:15–16.
7. Fong, *Racial Equality*, 80.

1 + 1 = 1

The text of Scripture provides a picture of a growing church looking different from what church growth principles espouse. As Donald McGavran puts it, "Men like to become Christians without crossing racial, linguistic or class barriers. . . . The principle is also readily discerned when it comes to pronounced class and racial barriers. It takes no great acumen to see that when marked differences of color, stature, income, cleanliness, and education are present, men understand the Gospel better when expounded by their own kind of people. They prefer to join churches whose members look, talk, and act like themselves."[8]

The suggested efficacy of homogeneous churches to win people to Christ, compared to heterogeneous congregations, assumes homogeneity is the primary reason people initially attend church. Yet, given the nature of the salvation message, the love of God and others seems more persuasive.[9] Jesus, on behalf of the triune God, embraces "outsiders" on the cross. Miroslav Volf describes God's love this way:

> Humanity is, however, not just the other of God, but the beloved other who has become an enemy. When God sets out to embrace the enemy, the result is the cross. On the cross the dancing circle[10] of self-giving and mutually indwelling divine persons opens up for the enemy; in the agony of the passion the movement stops for a brief moment and a fissure appears so that sinful humanity can join in (see John 17:21). We, the others—we, the enemies—are embraced by the divine persons who love us with the same love with which they love each other and therefore make space for us within their own eternal embrace.[11]

The heterogeneous nature of multiracial congregations is a tangible expression of the love of God that accepts and welcomes diverse peoples to a common fellowship.[12] Michael Emerson, writing about Wilcrest Baptist church, observed this characteristic: "For whites and American-born blacks, Dr. Woo said they often are attracted to the diversity because they

---

8. McGavran, *Church Growth*, 227.

9. In Luke 19, Zacchaeus the tax-collector is loved and accepted by Jesus. Grace, in spite of sin, brought Zacchaeus into the kingdom of God.

10. Long, "Periochoresis (Circumincession)," line 1. This dance, referred to as *periochoresis*, is the interactive relationship between God the Father, Son, and Spirit.

11. Volf, *Exclusion*, 128–29.

12. See Paul's admonition of Peter in Galatians 2 over Peter's conduct with the Gentile believers. The truth of the gospel Paul appeals to is the one that has united Jews and Gentiles in Christ.

themselves feel ostracized. He noted that they are often divorced, single parents, alcoholics, and drug addicts, people who have come from broken homes, released inmates, and people whose lives have been scarred by neglect. As some members told me in interviews, they believed that if Wilcrest was open enough to accept racial diversity, it might also be open to accept them."[13]

The church, being destined to have members who are from "every nation, from all tribes and peoples and languages,"[14] affirms the importance of heterogeneous churches striving to emulate the eternal church—what the church will be justifies pursuing it now.[15] Kathleen Garces-Foley observes, "Multiethnic churches are a human attempt to create the kind of perfected church that Jesus will complete upon his Second Coming."[16]

The Homogeneous Unit Principle (HUP)

Both HUP and mutual acceptance[17] congregations are products of God's people being led to pursue particular perspectives on introducing Christ to non-believers. These methods of church ministry are not at odds in advocating for Christ, although the manner in which they attempt this is different. It might be more appropriate to understand them as part of a spectrum of ministry styles. Both viewpoints strive to meet people where they are, and serve people in their areas of perceived need.

The Scriptures describe both HUP and mutual acceptance churches as familiar forms of ministry. The early church, as described in Acts and some of Paul's letters, indicates that congregations comprised of mainly Jews were healthy and thriving. Critiquing the HUP is not to suggest it is less biblical. The HUP can, however, in the interest of expedience, overlook the integrated dynamic of the Body of Christ.

---

13. Emerson and Woo, *People,* 109.

14. Rev 7:9

15. Matt 6:10—We are to desire and pray that God's will is done here on earth as it is in Heaven.

16. Garces-Foley, *Crossing,* 39.

17. "Mutual acceptance" is the concept that all who have been brought into the Body of Christ are welcome in the Body of Christ. Fong writes, "Each congregation of professing confessing Christians should reflect in visible form an attitude of mutual acceptance for all who come to the grace that Christ offers to all in the world regardless of race, class or language. The multi-racial, multi-class church becomes a testimony to the world what the grace of God can do" (Fong, *Racial Equality,* 120.).

Proponents of the HUP are not racist nor do they condone the sin that justifies segregation. They justifiably argue that homogeneous congregations meet unregenerate hearts where they are at, and Jesus will bring them around in due time. Quoting from Gerald Palmer, Wagner points out, "we must be willing to start churches that are homogeneous in nature if this is the best way to reach people and help them begin the journey of fellowship with other believers. . . . [T]he homogeneous unit is a spiritual and effective way of beginning and moving a group toward a heterogeneous scriptural ideal."[18] In other words, HUP proponents do not expect non-Christians to act like Christians.

The HUP is sensitive to unregenerate human nature. Neil Postman argues that the issue of race has been a concern in the United States for a while. He reports that in the middle of the nineteenth century, the question was raised: "Is it possible to have a coherent, stable culture made of people of different languages, religions, traditions, and races?"[19] This thought caused fear in people and prompted them to act in what we would now deem an irrational manner.[20] Postman maintains that this blending of cultures is an ongoing social experiment. Based on what he describes, it seems to this author, that churches with a HUP-influenced approach minister to those who do not wish to participate in this social experiment.[21]

C. Peter Wagner states, "No one involved wants to sacrifice the cultural mandate, but if it is necessary to settle for something short of the ideal in order to bring new people into the kingdom of God, then it is proper to make the sacrifice."[22] That said, HUP proponents face the challenge of balancing "living kingdom values" against "what works." Of course, they do not advocate racism or classism to introduce non-believers to Christ.[23] Even if one disagrees with a HUP approach, demonizing its position neither offers a solution nor wins its proponents over if constructive dialogue is the goal.

18. Wagner, *Growth and Gospel*, 168.
19. Postman, *Education*, 135–36.
20. Postman points out, "T. S. Eliot was so frightened at the thought he moved to England and stayed there. (ibid., 136)"
21. Churches' rationale for avoiding racial integration is a subject beyond the scope of this project. Postman's point is raised to show that the secular world understands the tension of intercultural relationships, too.
22. Wagner, *Growth and Gospel*, 170.
23. Stetzer, *Planting*, 184–85.

It is important to further note that homogeneity is not restricted to race. It encompasses age, education, class, income, cultural interests, and language. At some level, people prefer to be with those like them. David Hesselgrave, commenting about social structures found inside the church, states, "There is no getting away from the fact that though there are many multiclass, multiethnic, multilingual churches, most churches tend to be class, caste, ethnic, or tribal churches in addition to being Christian churches!"[24]

Change and Conflict Management

Now I appeal to Euodia and Syntyche. Please, because you belong to the Lord, settle your disagreement. And I ask you, my true partner, to help these two women, for they worked hard with me in telling others the Good News. (Phil 4:2–3, NLT)

The process of going from one race and cultural perspective to two or more is tough. Thinking that joining congregations across racial lines will be "easy" because all the people involved love Christ is idyllic but hardly realistic. The book of Acts shows how apostolic church leadership possesses humanity like our own in their interaction with others.[25] Paul's confrontation of Peter[26] over his conduct with Gentiles shows that the new relationship between Jew and Gentile is going to take work.

What will it take to create a healthy union between churches? An absence of conflict does not necessarily indicate that all things are well. Conflict may be absent because it is being avoided, there is a lack of awareness that something is wrong, or problems manifest themselves in ways other than conflict. When churches plan to join together, they need a biblical understanding of conflict engagement and resolution in their proverbial toolbox.[27]

Jesus outlines a means for resolving conflict in Matt 18, and Paul provides a hint of how this process functions in Phil 4. Apparently, two women, Euodia and Syntyche, are not getting along. They share a common bond in Christ, yet are at odds and in need of reconciliation. Paul asks

---

24. Hesselgrave, *Cross-Culturally*, 116.
25. Paul and Barnabas in Acts 15:36–39.
26. Gal 2:11–14
27. For further discussion on conflict management, *The Peacemaker* by Ken Sande is an excellent resource.

intermediaries, people who know both women, to assist with the resolution of their disagreement.[28] The local Body of Christ has a redemptive role in bringing about restoration of relationships within the Community of Christ—a crucial component when joining congregations together.

Shepherding a congregation through change can be a trying ordeal. Preparing a congregation to exchange its identity for another, involving people they hardly know, is a step toward the unknown and uncomfortable.

Looking again in Acts, the leadership brings the Jerusalem church through both conflict and change. In Acts 6, the apostles minister to the Hellenistic Jewish widows by appointing others[29] who assist with their care—prototypes of deacons are appointed to leadership roles. In Acts 15, the apostles and elders defuse a contentious issue—Gentiles are acknowledged as co-heirs and brethren with Jews.

In both instances, change occurs after conflict. This is not to say that conflict instigates change, but circumstances that have the potential to cause conflict can facilitate change. The resolution of conflict and acceptance of change was based on trust—the people of God trusted the leadership God had put in place.[30]

Reviving the Body of Christ through Unity

By this all people will know that you are my disciples, if you have love for one another. (John 13:35, ESV)

Is the Body of Christ Ailing?

According to a 2008 study, approximately 1 percent of all congregations in the United States close their doors each year.[31] A more in-depth study reports that the number of churches that close their doors is only marginally

---

28. Perhaps Paul's advice reveals something about the personal disagreement and experience he had with Barnabas over John Mark, as reported in Acts 15. It is plausible to suspect that friends of both Paul and John Mark (cf. 2 Tim 4:11) were instrumental in bringing about reconciliation between them.

29. Commentaries observe that there were six Jews with Hellenized names and a Gentile proselyte.

30. An expression of Heb 13:17—leaders are acting on behalf of God for the welfare of His people.

31. Banks, "Study," line 1.

A Challenge to the Status Quo

less than the number of new churches started. David Olson observed that there was only a net gain of 300 churches per year between 2000–2005. His findings suggest, "there needs to be a yearly net gain of 3,205 churches to keep up with American population growth. This number is ten times higher than the actual net gain."[32]

A church's demise may come about from any number of factors. Church closure may stem from congregants lost through conflict over doctrinal issues, an aging population, unfilled leadership posts, unmet expectations about the church's ministry, discord over issues of personal preference, and/or demographic change. A decline in those associating or identifying with Christianity is also slowing the church's growth.[33] Whatever the reasons, most, if not all, Christians would agree that the end of a local body of Christ can reflect poorly on Christ.

Along the lines of a closing church, church bodies that fragment through dissension also erode the Body of Christ. Kim Simmons states, "church splits communicate negative things: Christians cannot get along; the church is a bunch of hypocrites; the Bible divides people. The long term result is that people confuse man's struggles with God's reputation."[34]

Join Congregations Together to Restore Health to the Body

If a church is headed for closure, what is a viable solution to prevent its end? Revitalizing or transforming a dying congregation is a sensible course of action.[35] Another option worth considering is merging congregations together. While merging can trigger a negative association with the corporate business environment, it captures an idea with which people are familiar. An apt metaphor to help people understand the process is helpful and better for a ministry setting. Given the nature of relationships between people and their church home, a biblical metaphor could ease an already stressful situation and process.[36]

In discussing merged church congregations, church consultant Terry Foland provides a helpful description of this concept:

---

32. Olson, *Crisis*, 120.
33. Zoll, "More Americans," line 2.
34. Simmons, *Merge Split*, 3.
35. Olson, *Crisis*, 136.
36. The discussion on possible metaphors for integrating congregations is found in chapter 6.

> Merger should not be viewed as a last-ditch effort to keep a struggling congregation open; rather, merger should clearly be the result of members' discerning what God is calling them to be and do and an effort to carry out an exciting new vision of the church.
>
> Merging congregations might seem to be a simple matter of getting together and working out some agreements that will make them one church. But the reality is that many underlying issues, emotions, and practical problems make the process of merging churches a complex and often exasperating enterprise. Merger is not about deciding to work together as a way that allows each congregation to continue as a distinct entity. Nor is it about one congregation being subsumed by another. Merger means closing each congregation in order that a new congregation may be birthed.[37]

While church merges seem to frequently involve hurting, stagnant or dying congregations, it can be forward-thinking rather than an act of desperation.

From a scriptural perspective, churches that join together can be a tangible expression of Jesus' prayer for unity amongst his people in John 17. Just as a wedding does not make a marriage, congregations that become one are not necessarily united. A successful union is when "the new church is characterized by trust, unity and spiritual health. It has become difficult or impossible to find groups within the new congregation that continue to identify themselves with any pre-merger church."[38]

---

37. Foland, *Beginning*, 64.
38. Laribee, *Factors*, 75.

3

What Others Say and Think

THIS CHAPTER EXAMINES AND summarizes key findings in the research and written works of seemingly unrelated issues (the multiracial church, change and conflict management, and church mergers) to create a foundation for bringing congregations together in a multiracial setting.

Making a Ministry Multiracial

What does it take to develop a multiracial ministry? Because people prefer to worship with people like themselves, multiracial churches do not suddenly appear. If the default for church attendance is a path of least resistance, then attending a church where relationships cross racial lines infers there is work to be done. To break the tendency of preference, deliberate steps are necessary to promote a multiracial congregation.

There are three books worth noting concerning multiracial ministry—*One Body, One Spirit*; *People of the Dream*; and *Building a Healthy Multiethnic Church*.

Creating a multiracial church is a worthwhile endeavor, and hardly something that comes about without being deliberate. *One Body, One Spirit* offers readers a helpful start for tackling such a venture. Based on the results of a nationwide survey, Yancey presents "seven principles that are important to the formation and maintenance of multiracial churches."[1] He notes that these do not guarantee success, but are components that contribute significantly to the health of a church ministering across race.

---

1. Yancey, *One Body*, 66.

1 + 1 = 1

As one of the researchers who designed the national study, Yancey is intimately familiar with the data collected and his findings are accessible to the non-academic. He gives a historical and biblical rationale for multiracial congregations and discusses the prevailing perspective on how to operate a multiracial church. He describes principles that facilitate this type of ministry. In brief, they are:

1. Inclusive worship—"worship that includes the cultural elements of more than one racial group."[2] Worship not limited to a style representing the majority population of the congregation conveys an attitude of acceptance, as opposed to assimilation. Worship goes beyond music—it "includes the way a church decorates its sanctuary, the preaching style of the pastor and the organization of the program."[3]

2. Diverse leadership—leadership that is multiracial conveys acceptance and a willingness to share power.[4] People in the racial minority want to see if there are leaders who can relate to them. Diverse leadership tells the congregation that there is relationship and a partnership to minister to all congregants.

3. An overarching goal—being multiracial is not an end unto itself. Rather, it is the product of the vision and primary motivation for the existence of the church. "[E]fforts to become multiracial should be in the context of the larger goals of the church."[5]

4. Intentionality—it takes effort to cultivate and sustain a multiracial environment. "Intentionality is the attitude that one is not going to just allow a multiracial atmosphere to develop but is going to take deliberate steps to produce that atmosphere."[6]

5. Personal skills—church leaders presiding over a multiracial ministry need interpersonal skills that are sensitive to the needs of congregants, patient in navigating inevitable conflict, able to relate across race and culture, and prepared to equip church members to live in an integrated, multiracial environment.

2. Ibid., 67.
3. Ibid., 82.
4. Ibid., 97.
5. Ibid., 101.
6. Ibid., 68.

6. Location—geographic proximity to the racial groups a church is trying to reach is an important variable. In reality, there are social factors that lead to the segregation of churches based on location. Churches with financial resources appear to physically follow their donor base, relocating a ministry to accommodate their congregation's preferences. Multiracial churches are more likely to succeed when there is a nearby racially diverse populace from which to draw. "Churches in neighborhoods that are closer to people of different races have an easier time becoming multiracial."[7]

7. Adaptability—because change is more likely to be a constant in a racially integrated church, leadership should equip their congregation for flexibility to accommodate the people who come through their doors. Racial integration gives God's people the opportunity to "discover" God from a different perspective.

Yancey's principles are derived from observations made about churches that are "successfully" multiracial. They are not exclusive, but are relevant gleanings from a sound research methodology. An emerging multiracial church cannot completely overhaul itself to accommodate new racial groups, but the members would do well to learn how to adapt to these new attendees if they want to keep them.[8]

Michael Emerson was the principal researcher of the study upon which George Yancey based his book. *People of the Dream* enhances the study by examining the ministry of one multiracial church. A unique aspect of this focused investigation is that Emerson is a member of the ministry he investigates. While this relationship introduces the potential for bias, this approach has the added benefit of intimate awareness with what works and what does not.

Emerson weaves the experiences of Wilcrest Baptist Church into the research findings of his national study. The participation in the book of Rodney Woo, senior pastor of the church, brings a significant dimension to the text. Together, Emerson and Woo offer a story that puts flesh on a body of research by giving readers a picture and example of what is going on—"the research shows this and this is what we have seen in the church." The story of Wilcrest is not confined to the research project, and there is ample

---

7. Ibid., 136.
8. Ibid., 140.

explanation of the history of the church that allows readers to understand how the church became what it is today.

Using the same data as Yancey, Emerson provides additional conclusions on the principles that sustain a multiracial ministry.[9] He suggests that a healthy multiracial ministry is one where:

1. An institutional commitment to racial equity is clearly stated—racial integration is not limited to representation, but is characterized by equality, shared power.

2. Leaders are personally deeply committed to racial equity—leaders purposely and faithfully pursue racial equity.

3. A common purpose supersedes racial equity—having racial equity is an outgrowth of their faith pursuit. In pursuit of the values of the church, racial diversity is an expression and by-product of faith.

4. Structures ensure racial equity—the organizational arrangement of the church is aligned to fulfill its value of racial equity.

5. There are internal forums, education, and groups—communication flows freely. "There must be space where issues can be talked about, people can learn about race issues, and misuses of power can be discussed."[10]

6. Leaders orchestrate the ministry environment—like the fictional creator and director, Christof, of the movie, *The Truman Show*, leaders monitor the environment of their ministry to keep things on track.

7. It is understood that people are at different places, and need help to move forward—people's understanding of a multiracial church spans a continuum and their commitment to the ministry's values will be indicative of what they comprehend. Becoming an advocate of racial equity is a process.

Emerson & Woo point out that forming a multiracial church is to proactively foster racial integration. Furthermore, to change a congregation with an identity, a history, an established structure, well defined networks, and a unique culture requires immense effort and excellent leadership skills, and involves a continual effort to gain the support of the congregation.[11]

---

9. Emerson and Woo, *People*, 168–69.
10. Ibid., 169.
11. Ibid., 166.

Leadership needs to be intentional and lead the congregation to its intended ministry vision.

In *Building a Healthy Multiethnic Church*, Mark DeYmaz offers his perspective on what it takes to sustain a multiethnic (his preferred term) church. He suggests that these churches ought to:

1. Embrace dependence [on God]. "The multiethnic church is a work of the Holy Spirit and of faith that cannot otherwise be attained through human means or methods."[12] A multiethnic church must be a work of God and can only come about as the result of God calling his people to form a multiethnic congregation.

2. Take intentional steps. Creating a multiethnic ministry takes work.

   > In order to build a healthy multiethnic church then, we must own up to our fears, insecurities, and concerns. . . . [W]e cannot allow our past experiences, personal preferences, or personalities, or those things with which we are most comfortable or that we can more easily control, to dictate what we do and how we do it. For if we acquiesce, we will surely build a church filled with others like us. Rather, we should take intentional steps to draw others in, and not only to accept or assimilate them into our local fellowships but to go one step further. We must learn to accommodate them.[13]

3. Empower diverse leadership. Diversity in a multiethnic church is promoted when the ethnic minorities see people like them in positions of leadership. This does not mean that quotas are being met or diversity is being enforced for the sake of diversity. Integration is encouraged because there is value in what others with a different perspective from the majority population bring to the ministry. Diverse leadership expresses both value and commitment to multi-ethnicity.

4. Develop cross-cultural relationships. The congregation needs to participate in the formation of relationships across racial and ethnic lines because it expresses commitment toward relationship. As DeYmaz puts it, "Cross-cultural relationships form the very foundation and fabric of a multiethnic church because trust is not a commodity so easily assumed in an environment where people must interact with others different from themselves."[14]

12. DeYmaz, *Building*, 47.
13. Ibid., 59.
14. Ibid., 84.

5. Pursue cross-cultural competence. Cross-cultural relationships are not limited to making friends with people who are different; they involve being sensitive to, learning about and appreciating perspectives distinct from our own.[15] Furthermore, leadership needs to care for ethnic and racial minorities, understanding that they are at various points along a continuum of comfort with other racial minorities and the racial majority culture. The maturity it takes to appreciate and respect backgrounds different from one's own is dependent on what the Holy Spirit is doing within that person.

6. Promote a spirit of inclusion. Inclusion allows diversity to find its expression in the ministry of the church. Inclusive ministry recognizes that people bring their various backgrounds to the church and allows this to inform how ministry is done. It includes music style, language, decorations, and the recognition of special days. It is an attitude of hospitality that minimizes barriers and fosters an environment where people from all walks of life feel welcome.[16]

7. Mobilize for impact. Finally, a multiethnic ministry is going to take action. It puts on display what God has made, and actively participates in the Great Commission.

Taking these three works and comparing them to one another, we can observe what characteristics are important to sustain a multiracial congregation in Figure 3.1.

The Experience of Creating and Sustaining a Multiracial Church

In addition to the principles described by Yancey, Emerson & Woo, and DeYmaz, what do other ministry practitioners have to say about multiracial ministry? Are there other characteristics distinctive for establishing a multiracial church? Compared to what has been touched on about Wilcrest Baptist and Mosaic of Central Arkansas, this section considers two churches in California offering two additional perspectives on fostering a multiracial environment.

---

15. Ibid., 96.
16. Ibid., 115.

Figure 3.1—Principles for a Multiracial Church

One Body, One Spirit	People of the Dream	Building a Healthy Multi ethnic Church
Inclusive worship	Institutional commitment to racial equity	Embrace dependence
Diverse leadership	Leaders committed to racial equity	Take intentional steps
An overarching goal	Common purpose exceeds racial equity	Empower diverse leadership
Intentionality	Structures ensure racial equity	Develop cross-cultural relationships
Personal skills	Talk about race issues	Pursue cross-cultural competence
Location	Be a DJ	Promote a Spirit of inclusion
Adaptability	Recognize people are at different places	Mobilize for impact

Mosaic Church, Los Angeles, California.

Gerardo Marti describes his experience at Mosaic in Los Angeles in his book, *A Mosaic of Believers*. As a member of the pastoral staff, Marti had intimate access to and familiarity with "behind-the-scenes" motivations and drivers of the ministry.

Multiethnicity is not Mosaic's primary intention and goal. "Mosaic's first and primary core value is mission: Mission is why the church exists. . . . [T]he church is not for Christians. The church is to participate with God in redeeming people."[17] Succinctly, "the focus of Mosaic's mission is evangelism."[18] How their evangelism ministry takes shape is a product of the mission field Mosaic inhabits.

Mosaic ministers to its community in ways that are understandable and relevant to the surrounding culture.[19] Its mission field determines the environment it is creating—in order to be hospitable to the people they

---

17. Marti, *Mosaic*, 75.
18. Ibid., 76.
19. Ibid., 68.

are trying to reach, it creates a place in which they would feel welcome.[20] "Because Mosaic draws artistically oriented people from various ethnicities, the creative arts at Mosaic provide a productive place for ethnic and racial blending."[21] Mosaic's ministry environment encourages diversity and attracts people of various backgrounds to a common purpose.

Mosaic's diversity is a product of its ministry philosophy. As Marti describes it, "Instead of targeting ethnic groups, Mosaic became multiethnic as a by-product of innovatively creating inclusive arenas that make ethnic identity irrelevant—or at least much less relevant. Multi-layered personal identities are accessed through one or more havens that emerge from innovations charismatic leaders enact in response to a changing social environment. Interpersonal interaction in the context of attractive arenas of involvement facilitates the strategic work of managing and reconstructing identity toward a common mission."[22] In other words, Mosaic is diverse because it has encouraged a setting that appeals to people across ethnic boundaries. Congregants do not attend Mosaic because it addresses specific ethnic needs, but for reasons other than ethnicity.

What type of environment promotes multiethnicity? Mosaic has formed what Marti terms a "haven." This concept describes "a refuge or sanctuary for a significant aspect of their religious desires, personal identities, and value systems."[23] These havens are Mosaic's expression of ministry—how it lives out faith. The havens are described as five distinct fields—theological, artistic, innovator, age and ethnic. Again, from Marti, "These five havens are the relational spaces for communal activity at Mosaic."[24]

Mosaic's distinctives, as described by Marti, reflect a type of ministry niche for the church. Mosaic has articulated its values and states them in language accessible to the community of people it is trying to introduce to Christ.[25] The havens express the values of Mosaic in ministry areas that the church invites people to participate.

20. Ibid., 89.
21. Ibid., 90.
22. Ibid., 181.
23. Ibid., 6.
24. Ibid., 7.
25. Mosaic's core values or metaphors are "**Wind** (Commission)—Mission is why the Church exists. The Church is a movement, not an institution. Every follower of Jesus is commissioned by God; **Water** (Community)—Love is the context for all mission. The Church is relational, not programmatic. Every follower of Jesus is part of a larger

Mosaic does not overtly address issues of race and ethnicity in its ministry. Marti explains,

> Ethnic transcendence, superseding ethnic identity in favor of other identities, is the strategy most consistently and most explicitly found at Mosaic. Spiritual leaders construct a new, inclusive "Christian" identity that redefines relationships between people of different ethnicities. . . . Therefore, in interaction with potential followers, leaders in multiethnic churches like Mosaic find some ground for status by which to transcend identity on a base of affinity and legitimacy. Status honor, whether claimed through shared ethnic membership or another means, undergirds the legitimacy necessary for the reorientation of identity based on a common corporate mission.
> A common identity begins with a base of affinity.[26]

Mosaic's attraction is consistent with the HUP in that there are common affinities that bring people to their church. As Marti puts it, "People at Mosaic did not join the congregation merely because it is the antithesis of places they did not like. My respondents indicated that they would rather not attend church at all than simply come to a church because it was 'less bad' than a past experience. Their explanations point to something much more subtle. Organizational diversity like that found at Mosaic requires people to cultivate bases of affinity which are inherently attractive."[27] Homogeneity at Mosaic manifests itself in an affinity other than race.

Mosaic's approach to racial reconciliation is in line with its view on ethnic transcendence. Its perspective is that "racial reconciliation is possible when church leaders recognize that members of ethnic and racial groups can participate in subcultures where racial differences are relatively unimportant." Marti continues, "In order to overcome racial differences, churches may have to establish or co-opt several subcultures that will still inevitably exclude individuals on a base other than race or ethnicity."[28]

---

community; **Wood** (Connection)—Structure must always submit to Spirit. The Church is empowering, not controlling. Every follower of Jesus is called and connected uniquely to serve; **Fire** (Communion) Relevance to culture is not optional. The Church is incarnational, not esoteric. Every follower of Jesus celebrates communion with God; and **Earth** (Character)—Creativity is the natural result of spirituality. The Church is transforming, not conforming. Every follower of Jesus grows in Christ-like character."

26. Marti, *Mosaic*, 17.
27. Ibid., 6.
28. Ibid., 184.

A limitation of ethnic transcendence is that it seems to diminish the importance and value of ethnicity. Mosaic's "success" stems from "its activity in the context of a popular American culture accessible to English-speaking second- and third-generation immigrants living in Los Angeles. This culture is already accessible to young Caucasians, and its accessibility provides the church with the opportunity to become multiethnic. The children and grandchildren of immigrants assimilate into the segment of American culture most accessible to them: white popular culture. These ethnics are socialized into popular culture through readily accessible media channels, substituting it for their identification with their ancestral history."[29] The ethnic cultural dynamic is absorbed by a larger, monocultural mindset: white popular culture. While ethnic perspectives are appreciated in what they contribute, assimilation based on affinity to values, and not defined by race or ethnicity, occurs.

Given Mosaic's ethnic transcendence approach, it seems odd that Marti sees Mosaic providing a haven for ethnicity. In context, Marti sees these havens as a place "for" safety "from" danger. As far as ethnicity is concerned, Mosaic is a place for "second- and third- generation ethnics escaping from mono-ethnic home churches."[30] He adds, "Within the broadly Americanized culture of Mosaic, [the children of immigrants] find refuge for 'being' ethnic without having to 'act' ethnic."[31] It bears noting that exchanging ethnic culture for a new culture (i.e., "white pop culture") is not the same as adopting the "culture of Christ."

Evergreen Baptist, Rosemead, California.

Kathleen Garces-Foley describes how Evergreen Baptist transformed its congregation from a monoracial culture to a multiracial environment in *Crossing the Ethnic Divide*. Garces-Foley gives insights about change in a church that converts from a focus on ethnic identity, Asian, to a vision and desire for ethnic diversity. The author defines a multiethnic church as "an inclusive, ethnically diverse community."[32]

---

29. Ibid., 188.
30. Ibid., 10.
31. Ibid., 11.
32. Garces-Foley, *Crossing*, 15.

In contrast to Mosaic, Evergreen deliberately strives to become a racially diverse congregation.[33] The impetus for diversifying is based on the Scriptures and a desire for racial reconciliation.[34] Diversity issues are discussed throughout the organization through sermons, programs, ministry groups and church communications.[35] The senior pastor is committed to having an open dialogue with his congregation and inviting them into a conversation about the issues of race and reconciliation.[36]

Evergreen, like Mosaic, has a diverse community from which to draw, and their move toward multiethnicity was driven in part by the growing diversity of the surrounding populace.[37] However, being in the right location at the right time does not imply that diversification of the church will happen automatically. Creating an environment of diversity is intentional, and being diverse does not imply that there is integration. "However the ideal multiethnic church is imagined, it most certainly means more than occupying the same physical space, which can so easily replicate the divisions of the surrounding society."[38] Furthermore, Roger Greenway opines, "A true [multiethnic] congregation blends distinctive elements of various ethnic traditions in such a way that no single tradition predominates or suppresses others. Nor is the outcome such an 'osterized' mixture that nobody can tell one element from another."[39]

Evergreen became an inclusive community by promoting an environment willing and wanting to embrace those who are different. Garces-Foley writes, "What makes a church feel like a community is not that everyone is interacting with everyone else but that the potential exists to form a bond with any member. . . . Describing a church as "inclusive" is a way of emphatically stressing that members are open to forming supportive bonds with anyone who walks through the door."[40] The community Evergreen cultivated was inclusive in leadership, programs and rituals—"multiethnic churches must put their words into actions by institutionalizing them in

---

33. Ibid., 22–24.
34. Ibid., 26.
35. Ibid., 6.
36. Ibid., 48–53.
37. Ibid., 31.
38. Ibid., 5.
39. Quoted in ibid., 85.
40. Ibid., 87–88.

church structures, most importantly the leadership, programming and corporate worship."[41]

At Evergreen, this institutionalization occurs by encouraging qualified, non-Asian leadership in both paid and non-paid positions. At the time *Crossing the Ethnic Divide* was written, Evergreen staff was still predominantly Asian.[42] The church is aware that it has a ways to go, but it is proactively moving in a direction that is diverse.

In their ministry, "Evergreen has offered a variety of programs and events that address the vision of reconciliation."[43] In addition, the leadership is willing to evaluate its success and failure in pursuing racial equity. Garces-Foley reports that "a racial reconciliation research group was formed to evaluate the racial climate at Evergreen and make recommendations for educating and training the church. The group reported in the newsletter that while Evergreeners give a high priority to racial reconciliation, they have limited understanding of the concept."[44] Evergreen's appetite for self-examination is a serious commitment to pursuing diversity.

Evergreen encourages ethnic diversity in the public rituals of corporate worship—baptism, communion, and music. They understand that what people see communicates values. "For the non-Asian visitor trying to decide if he or she can fit in at Evergreen, the importance of seeing diversity 'up front' cannot be overstated."[45]

To explain how churches approach ethnic ministry, Garces-Foley describes strategies by which churches communicate the significance of ethnicity in their ministry—how ethnicity is viewed in a multiethnic church (Figure 3.2 represents this description). "Some churches ignore ethnic differences altogether, as in the color-blind approach, and impose the dominant group's culture on the church leadership style, program themes, and corporate worship. Others emphasize ethnic diversity publicly as a stated value but fail to institutionalize it in church structures, or conversely institutionalize diversity in structures without making it part of their public values. A fourth alternative is to insist on diversity of ethnic expression in every aspect of the institution."[46]

41. Ibid., 89.
42. Ibid., 90.
43. Ibid., 91.
44. Ibid., 92.
45. Ibid., 93.
46. Ibid., 95.

What Others Say and Think

Figure 3.2—Types of Multiethnic Congregations[47]

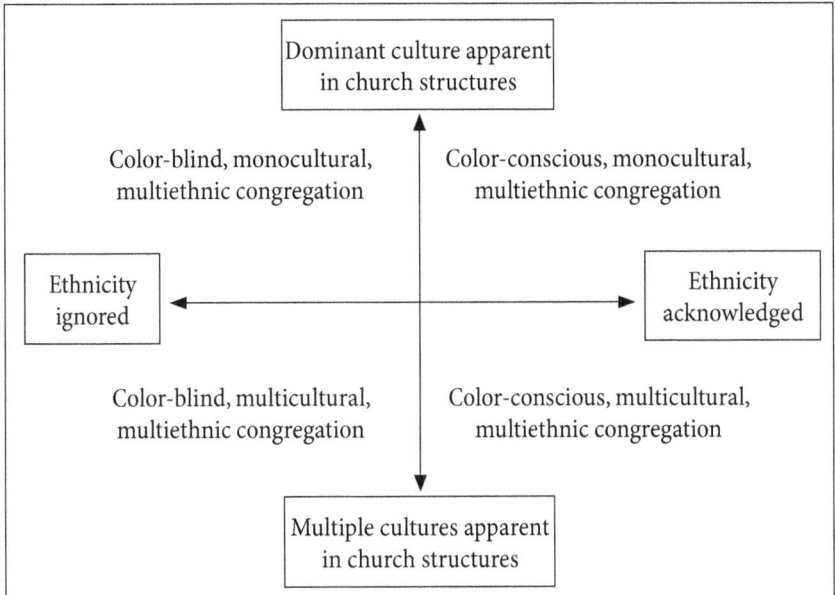

This matrix represents the prominence of ethnicity in a multiethnic church. She explains further, "These categories do not correspond perfectly to the way real churches are grappling with the question of how to frame ethnic identity in their congregation."[48] Where churches are in this matrix is dynamic. Some parts of their ministry may reflect different points on the continuum indicating that this is a process.

How ethnicity is viewed influences how ethnic issues are handled. For example, part of engaging ethnic and racial issues involves formulating a plan for dealing with conflict and, in particular, racial reconciliation. Garces-Foley observes that the "[o]ne thing all multiethnic churches have in common is that they are engaged with the question of how to frame diversity and inclusivity in their discourses, their interactions and their

---

47. Adapted from Garces-Foley's "Salience of Ethnic Identity in Church Culture," ibid., 95. This graphic is based on a table Garces-Foley uses to describe ethnic identity, representing a way to visualize her observation. *Crossing the Ethnic Divide* by Kathleen Garces-Foley (2007) Table 4.1 from p. 95 (adapted). By permission of Oxford University Press, Inc.

48. Ibid., 95.

institutional structures."⁴⁹ A church might make racial conflict and reconciliation issues part of their sermon series, keeping it at a theological level, as Mosaic does. Or a church might take the discussion deeper by inviting people to dialogue in a facilitated small group setting—an approach Evergreen utilizes.⁵⁰

While race is not an "issue" at Mosaic, Evergreen, in contrast, believes race is a relevant matter that needs to be discussed openly. "From the pulpit and in the newsletter, Ken [the pastor of Evergreen] keeps racial issues on the front burner as he encourages members to greater commitment to the church's vision statement. That vision, as Ken and others have presented it to the congregation, addresses not only the barriers that individuals construct between themselves and others, but the reality of racialization that transcends personal encounters."⁵¹ By keeping racial issues at the forefront, Evergreen is "color-conscious: publicly acknowledging the way in which social barriers are erected on the basis of one's skin color . . . acknowledging that ethnicity matters to Evergreeners as individuals. They are proud of their distinctive ethnic histories and cultures and do not want to live in a color-blind world that effaces ethnic differences."⁵² Evergreen creates a place for safe dialogue over a potentially divisive issue.

Dealing with Change and Conflict

"It isn't the changes that do you in, it's the transitions." The author continues, "Change is situational. . . . Transition, on the other hand, is psychological."⁵³ If the leadership of a church merger fails to prepare the congregations for change and transition, the fallout is that much greater because both churches are affected.

Manuel Ortiz observes that transforming one church into a multiracial ministry is a recognized challenge in itself.⁵⁴ It involves transitioning a congregation from what they have known, and inviting them into something different. Add another congregation going through the same process and the challenge multiplies. It will probably not be as simple as

49. Ibid., 101.
50. Ibid., 52.
51. Ibid., 49.
52. Ibid., 53.
53. Bridges, *Transitions*, 3.
54. Ortiz, *New People*. 145–48.

just taking two churches and working through differences stemming from race or ethnicity. Both congregations will have to work through issues such as doctrine, church governance, music, children's ministry, meeting time, location, staffing, leadership and finances.

A number of books about both conflict resolution and change management exist. While these topics have some overlap, they are distinct issues. For the discussion of this work, change management involves organizational change in the operations of an institution, whereas conflict resolution occurs between individuals. When changing the culture and dynamics of a church, the organizational change often gives rise to relational conflict. Interpersonal conflict can occur between and within (a) leadership teams, (b) congregants and leadership, and (c) congregants.

Lessons on Change from the Business Sector

In response to his book *Good to Great*, Jim Collins wrote a monograph specific to social sector organizations. He observed that the same timeless principles he discovered through research on the business sector are also applicable to the social and non-profit sector, including churches.[55] In some ways, merging congregations is not unlike joining together business corporations.[56]

David M. Dealy, speaking from years of business management experience, makes this observation about change:

> managing change is really managing others' expectations—shareholders and stakeholders in the firm. Not only do you have to manage those well, but you must also be aware of the limitations of others to manage expectations within their respective organizations. Do not be lulled into a sense of security because you believe you have managed other parties' expectations very well. You must make sure that they too "can and are" managing others' expectations well. Whether it is the CEO or the janitor who cleans your offices, you must understand that each and every individual inside and outside of your organization is managing expectations in their own way with their supervisors, peers, and subordinates.[57]

---

55. Collins, *Social Sectors*, 3.

56. As there are some similarities, the dissimilarities are no less significant. The church is not sustained by a profit motive, it has different values and measures of "success."

57. Dealy, *Change*, 89.

To translate to a church setting, change can be managed by helping congregants understand what is changing (manage their expectations) and how they can communicate this change to others (enabling them to manage the expectations of others).

It is no surprise that bringing about change is not easy. The bigger and more complex the change, the harder it can be to navigate and establish. Management expert, John Kotter states that change, in order to be successful, needs two important criteria: process and leadership.

First, useful change tends to be associated with a multistep process that creates power and motivation sufficient to overwhelm all the sources of inertia. Second, this process is never employed effectively unless it is driven by high-quality leadership, not just excellent management.[58] Kotter suggests there are eight stages for major change in transforming an organization.[59] These stages are:

1. Establish a sense of urgency.
2. Create the guiding coalition—the leaders who will guide the organization through change.
3. Develop a vision and strategy.
4. Communicate the change vision—what will the organization become.
5. Empower broad-based action—remove the barriers to change.
6. Generate short-term wins—help transition by creating attainable short-run goals, highlight gains, and rewarding participants.
7. Consolidate gains and produce more change—leverage credibility to initiate more change and strategically utilize allies and advocates.
8. Anchor new approaches in the culture—embed changes into the organizational ethos, process, and structure.

As noted previously, there are points of application in the corporate world that can be relevant in the church. Likewise, there are opinions to be ignored. For instance, Kotter proposes getting rid of obstacles to empower action, but when people within the family of God are obstacles over preferences or non-moral issues, they cannot simply be removed because they are hindering progress. Love and forbearance as described in Rom 14 and 15

---

58. Kotter, *Change*, 120.
59. Ibid., 21.

What Others Say and Think

have priority in relationships. Organizational expedience gives way to the Gospel imperative, "Love one another."[60]

In addition, change is not necessarily a "win-lose" proposition—if one side "wins," the other side "loses." In their book *Collaboration Handbook*, Michael Winer and Karen Ray provide a clear process for bringing about change that is beneficial to all involved ("win-win"). Their workbook is for organizations creating temporary work relationships in order to achieve a particular outcome that the organizations cannot attain individually.

Winer and Ray describe collaboration as "a mutually beneficial and well-defined relationship entered into by two or more organizations to achieve results they are more likely to achieve together than alone."[61] They note further that the benefits of the collaboration will be the fulfillment of organizational and/or individual self-interest.[62]

Their process entails four stages:

1. Envision results by working individual-to-individual. Leaders from the organizations involved create a vision and define desired outcomes for the collaboration. They start by building relationships of trust through common ground, sharing power, and getting to know one another.

2. Empower ourselves by working individual-to-organization. Leaders secure commitments for their respective organizations, work through points of conflict, share the responsibilities between groups, and work through the decision-making process that will impact the participants.

3. Ensure success by working organization-to-organization. Both organizations and all their people tackle the work together. Everyone ultimately agrees on what is to be done and understands the measurable benchmarks of their vision and goals.

4. Endow continuity by working collaboration-to-community. The goal has been attained. The impacted community continues the work started and the temporary collaboration comes to a close.

The outcome is different for a church merge because it is a permanent relationship. By way of impact, with the redemptive gospel message in mind, the church leads and participates in interracial conversations and relationships as part of a larger community.

60. John 13:34–35
61. Winer and Ray, *Collaboration*, 24.
62. Ibid., 27.

1 + 1 = 1

Managing Interpersonal Conflict

It has been said that when a person marries, they not only gain a spouse, they also acquire a new family. In a similar manner, when churches join together the complex web of interpersonal relationships grows, too.

In light of this, planning a healthy, simple process for dealing with the conflict to come is wise. It can be a formal procedure or more organic, where leadership openly models godly conflict resolution for the congregation.

Making Two Churches into One

As noted previously, marriage is an analogy for bringing churches together. Taking this comparison a further, it might be more appropriate to describe it as a marriage that creates a "blended family." How can leadership help the "new" siblings work through issues when they have a disagreement?

Simmons, in reference to bringing split congregations back together, observes that for a merge to be successful there must be agreement and harmony on fundamental issues—doctrine, philosophy of ministry, location and money.[63]

Simmons provides helpful insights[64] but lacks an element of critical analysis. Some assertions his sources make go unchallenged. Case in point, he accepts at face value a statement made that for a merger to be successful, "the social contexts of both congregations must be similar. If the people belong to different social or economic classes, for example, a merger will not work."[65] This allegation made by a source is unchallenged and Simmons does not test or demonstrate validity for the claim. In light of this project's work, the implications of this view are substantial. It suggests that racially heterogeneous congregations would not be candidates for successful integration.

Laribee gives five stages in merging and identifies things to be aware of as the churches move through the stages.[66] His work can unearth un-

---

63. Simmons, *Merge Split*, 175.

64. Simmons offers seven steps for the creation of the new church, including a feasibility study (steps 1 and 2) and implementation (steps 3 through 7). Simmons' steps are: 1—Making contact, 2—Exploring the specifics, 3—Catching the vision, 4—Becoming a team, 5—Resolving conflicts, 6—Presenting and voting on the merger, and 7—Merging

65. Simmons, *Merge Split*, 15.

66. While step-by-step guidelines are not part of this project's intent, it can be helpful to know what fundamental questions to ask when developing a new ministry created by a merge.

seen issues that might come up. These blind spots reveal that what could be one church's "no-brainer" may be another's "deal-breaker." Beyond good communications and conflict resolution that is safe and healthy, what should congregations be alert to?

The first stage evaluates whether or not a respective church's situation warrants a merger. It challenges leadership to understand their motives, leadership style, and church culture as well as the spiritual, organizational, and relational health of the congregation.[67]

The second stage is characterized by self-awareness and resolving the differences between congregations. As they work together, the representatives of each church should "negotiate until all parties find mutually beneficial solutions to those differences. The leadership must commit itself to delay proceeding until mutually beneficial solutions are found. Never make the fatal mistake of assuming details can be worked out later. . . . All parties must feel that these negotiated solutions are fair, right, mutually beneficial, and most importantly, desirable."[68] Congregations each examine their respective philosophy of ministry and expectations on how ministry will be done—what is non-negotiable and what is adaptable?

Organizationally, churches need to be alert to legal changes and how staff employment and/or resignations will be handled. While the life cycle of the church may continue on because of people and assets, there are aspects of the merge that can close the church such as the loss of leadership, power struggles and unresolved conflict.

In stage three, congregations are prepared for the next steps. Even if the merge does not take place, congregants still need to be debriefed and allowed to grieve the outcome. If the congregations move forward with the merge, they need time to anticipate what comes next. "[T]he leader must clearly and repeatedly remind themselves and their constituents that the primary purposes of successful mergers are to shatter the status quo, to irrevocably alter the congregations' values and the forms, norms and procedures that express those values, and especially to displace the leadership that represented the status quo and values."[69] Leadership must communicate and demonstrate foresight concerning what is coming, empathy for members' feelings, and a vision for God's call for the congregations. Articulating how life will change for the church will help the adjustment.

67. Laribee, *Factors*, 150–51.
68. Ibid., 153.
69. Ibid., 156.

Stages four and five span the transition period of the merger—decisions are made and plans executed. What was once a good idea now becomes reality. Stage five covers aspects of the merge that may be ignored because they are largely symbolic in nature. Rituals are important because they bring closure and allow new traditions to be introduced to facilitate building new relationships.[70]

The pastoral role is a distinct obstacle for both Simmons and Laribee. For Simmons, resolving who pastors the new congregation is part of the feasibility process. He recalls, "One of the first questions that came to my mind was whether both pastors would remain in the united church and if so how we would relate to each other. The pastors may decide to work together as co-pastors or as senior and associate. These options may be discussed by both pastors and leadership of both churches realizing the effect this may have on the congregation. The pastors should fully support any decision about their relationship. Otherwise, the merger could lead to a split."[71] The solution for their church was to create a co-pastorate.

Laribee is less optimistic about this type of arrangement. He advocates a complete change of leadership to ensure post-merger success.

> An essential factor that contributes to success of a merger is the resignation of the former leadership. Although all organizations resist change, they are more likely to change their values or expressions following a change in leadership. This is largely true because the leader tends to symbolize the life and values of the organization. The resignation of the ministers symbolizes to the congregation the loss of those old values and ways of being that the minister embodied. As long as the former ministers remain present, past values remain present in the organizational consciousness. This may be just as true for a leader who is not admired as for a leader who is very admired.
>
> In some churches, the life and values of the congregation of the may be symbolized in the church secretary, the youth minister, the chairperson of the governing board, or the patriarch of a powerful family. Whoever embodies the values and ways of the pre-merger church symbolizes the old congregational culture. The remaining presence of these persons impairs the ability of the congregation to adopt the new values and ways of being that a merger would form.

---

70. Ibid., 160–61.
71. Simmons, *Merge Split*, 31.

A common argument in favor of keeping the pre-merger leadership is to provide continuity during the transition. Unfortunately, continuity is the problem! Continuity of former ways, values and personnel provide the fuel that fires much post-merger conflict, friction and confusion.

Finally, many congregations seeking merger do so because of problems they cannot resolve by themselves. Not infrequently, these problems are the consequences of choices of the leaders. Sometimes the leaders resist the resolution of problems, and sometimes friends of leaders who loyally protect a leader's interests resist the resolution. In all of these situations, the continuing presence of the leader complicates the issue, and impairs the ability of the organization to resolve problems, both before and after the merger. The resignation of the minister, ministerial staff, and other powerful leaders that symbolize the past greatly increases the ability of the congregation to adapt and change, especially in a merger.[72]

Because merging churches shakes up the status quo and leadership, the merge should displace ineffective leaders and pastoral staff.[73] Because church mergers are for saving dying congregations rather than a proactive approach to ministry, he cautions that not getting rid of the pastoral staff will perpetuate the problem.[74] While seeming to be utilitarian and callous, Laribee knows that changing leadership impacts people, and understands that ministry is about people. As a result, consideration and implementation of these changes must be weighed carefully.

The strength of Laribee's work is his emphasis on critical self-analysis—What do both congregations bring to the table (pro and con), and how will they resolve their differences? However, the study is mainly informed by materials written from a business viewpoint, and the interaction with Scripture is limited.

On the flip side, Laribee's model has two significant weaknesses. First, it treats the church as a business suggesting that to fix the problem one needs to get rid of the people (opposition). This approach contradicts the redemptive message of the gospel. Laribee does not discuss or consider the possibility of a change of heart. Second, joining congregations together, especially from a multiracial perspective, is not a business decision. Where

72. Laribee, *Factors*, 82–83.
73. Laribee, *Factors*, 114.
74. Ibid., 114–15.

intercultural friendships are at stake, uniting congregations is a relationship between equal partners.

Laribee, Carol Gregg, and Kelly McClendon offer assistance for merging congregations and their understanding of the process is helpful. Yet merges across race or ethnicity are not addressed. Their omission may be simply because the idea never occurred to them.

Both Gregg and Mariko Yanagihara build on Laribee's work by offering guidelines as well incorporating some of his observations.[75] Gregg's study of mergers provides an overview and beginning point for exploring a merge. Gregg presents a map for attaining a successful merge. She describes ingredients for a good merge—motives, obstacles and recommendations.

Very little has been written about church mergers that create multiracial ministry.[76] The biblical basis has received scant attention, and the practical challenges need fleshing out. This work seeks to start and expand the discussion.

A Note on Multi-Site Expansion

One particular type of church merger that creates a multiracial ministry follows the multi-site expansion model. "Multi-site ministry," involves a single, parent church ministering at multiple locations. The concept behind a multi-site church is that it is one church with multiple locations, or as one proponent describes, "one church (meaning one staff, one board, one budget) meeting in multiple locations, usually with the various sites developing unique personalities yet sharing the same 'brand identity' and DNA."[77]

This ministry movement has been growing in popularity and one method it employs for expansion is merging—establishing a new campus[78] by merging with another church.[79] Using a business-world description, this would more aptly be described as an acquisition or take-over.[80] One church

---

75. However, both fail to interact with his work.

76. Two works to reference are found in the bibliography under Priest & Priest and Yanagihara.

77. Ferguson, "Multi-Site," lines 4–8.

78. Churches using a multi-site strategy commonly refer to their locations as campuses.

79. Tomberlin. "Churches Embrace," lines 1–2

80. This description of a "multi-site merge" is an observation, not a value statement. Additionally, this definition of a merge contrasts what was described earlier by Foland.

describes the process of merging with another church in this way (humor presumed): "Early in the conversation, we review ten leading markers which are common commitments. Later in the conversation, we outlined terms of surrender".[81]

An underlying principle for this type of merge is that there is an established approach for conducting ministry.[82] Multi-site churches are driven by a parent church responsible for setting the vision and philosophy of ministry for all of its campuses (daughter churches). Using corporate parlance, it is like a franchise[83] or a subsidiary. In contrast, "A true merger takes place when two corporations combine so thoroughly that neither of the participants survives legally. What emerges is an entirely new entity, with a new name, structure, line of products and services, culture and so on."[84]

In relation to multiracial churches, this "acquisition" approach has the promise to be effective because the potential for some types of conflict is minimized. However, by definition, a multi-site ministry maintains its DNA—vision, mission, core values, and culture. If a single-race congregation acquires/takes over a congregation of a different race with the hope of creating a diverse environment, values and practices (e.g., leadership, corporate worship, philosophy of ministry, identity) will need to change in order for the new church to keep the members of minority race.

A significant challenge to the multi-site method of developing a church is that it has a primary prevailing vision. By virtue of this approach, it focuses on a "brand" and "proven" style of conducting church. A "one-dominant perspective" would appear to be incompatible with multiracial ministry, if homogeneity is the aim.[85] Furthermore, an inflexible attitude toward culture, as determined by race, will doom any multiracial ministry trying to rise out of a single race environment.

It would be "easier" for a minority race congregation to takeover an Anglo congregation than the reverse. Because of historical and perceived notions of power, an Anglo congregation submitting to a minority race

81. Bird, "Forum *Meeting Notes*." The document cited are meeting notes taken and graciously provided by Dr. Warren Bird, Research Director with Leadership Network.

82. Congregations that merge with a multi-site church have bought into/need to buy into what the "mother" church is doing. There are some negotiables but a non-negotiable is the philosophy of ministry (DNA) for the multi-site ministry. "If you're willing to do things the way we have successfully done them . . ."

83. Nelson, "Mega, Schmega,", 64–68.

84. Arsenault, *Forging*, 84.

85. A discussion about assimilation follows in chapter 6.

congregation makes things easier. Pastor David Anderson relates a story where an African-American pastor gained an influx of Anglo congregants and was bewildered by their presence. This pastor said, "White people are coming to my church and I don't know what to do." The fears the pastor had were unfounded because it turned out that the new congregants "were at this black church to submit, to grow, and to learn, not to take over."[86]

A multiracial congregation taking over a single-race congregation would be much more likely to succeed. A multiracial congregation has already demonstrated that it values people across races. Bringing a single-race congregation under their care would be an expansion of what they already do and an outgrowth of what they value. Two churches surveyed, The Journey and Fellowship of Faith, provide examples of how this can succeed.

Mark DeYmaz's congregation in Little Rock, Arkansas, Mosaic Church, has experienced this type of success as well. DeYmaz reports that they enfolded a Latino congregation into their multiracial church community.[87]

Furthermore, Warren Bird, in response to a question about multi-site mergers that create multiracial church communities, says, "My prediction is that it will happen through mergers. Our multi-site survey also asked, 'Have you used your multi-site approach to assist (or take responsibility for) a declining church?' Of 197 churches that replied to this question, 30% said 'yes,' plus 10% more said, 'No, but we plan to in the future.' I think those mergers will open the way to more multi-ethnic congregations."[88] DeYmaz adds this thought to the conversation he was having with Bird: "I agree with Warren; and through our recent experience at Mosaic, we hope to both inspire and inform other local church pastors interested in merging churches in pursuit of the multi-ethnic vision."[89]

Responding to a question from this author about multiracial churches created from a merge, Bird writes, "It seems to me that merging is full of enough potholes within the same culture that few would venture across cultures. Churches have a hard enough time becoming multi-cultural themselves.... If you explore the main reasons churches merge—the most common theme being that one is significantly faltering—I doubt you'd find

---

86. Anderson, *Multicultural*, 45–47.

87. DeYmaz, "Expediting," lines 1–56.

88. This question asked was, "What's your sense between multi-ethnic churches and multi-ethnic campuses of multi-site churches? Which is more likely to take the lead, and why?" Bird believes multi-site churches will take the lead in establishing multiethnic churches. DeYmaz, "Expediting," lines 61–70.

89. DeYmaz, "Expediting," lines 71–73.

many examples of churches that try to learn a new skill (blending ethnicities) in the process."[90] Bird's experience seems to indicate that creating a multiracial ministry is hard enough as it is without trying to blend church cultures together through merging.

More churches will attempt to create a multiracial ministry. When it happens, I suspect that the multi-site merge approach will work best if a multiracial congregation adds a single-race congregation to its ministry, as DeYmaz's church did. The multi-site multiethnic church (as opposed to monoracial multi-site churches) will take the lead in starting multiethnic congregations.

If a single race multi-site ministry diversifies its leadership, develops a worship style that the minority congregation helps to shape, commits to intercultural relationships and racial justice, and alters its philosophy of ministry regarding race and ethnicity, then it will have a chance to advance God's kingdom as a multiracial ministry. If a multi-site ministry is not already multiracial or actively pursuing diversity, it will be difficult to turn a stated value into a realized ministry practice.

---

90. Personal correspondence with author.

4

Churches That Became Multiracial through Merging

CHURCHES THAT HAVE BEEN through the process of creating a multi-racial congregation by bringing together mono-racial assemblies complete my research on this topic. I contacted eight congregations in the Pacific Northwest that attempted this venture.[1] At least one key leader from each founding church was interviewed, and congregants were invited to participate in a survey on what they experienced. Of the eight, four of the churches had some congregants complete a survey. Based on available information, either through interviews, media coverage or surveys, six congregations contributed to this portion of the study. There were forty-one survey responses and fourteen interviews with ministry leaders. The interviews ranged from 30–90 minutes in length, and often provided background information and specific details about the churches.[2]

The survey offers an additional dimension to the literary research and interviews. The survey responses represent what people went through in the formation of their respective multiracial church communities.

The survey questions focus on:

- Demographics—church home, race, and familiarity with merge process

---

1. The churches were found through word of mouth and mass media.

2. Interview questions were: What did you learn through the process of bringing the respective churches together? What positive/benefit stands out to you? What negative/obstacle/challenge stands out to you? What would you have done again? What would you have done differently? Why is the racial/ethnic component of your church important? What advice would you give others who are considering doing what you have done?

- Church characteristics—racial make-up before and after merge (did the church really become multiracial?)
- Obstacles & challenges—awareness of potential conflict points, how difficulties were handled

The responses are considered in aggregate, as the number of completed surveys per congregation is too few to make a definitive statement about the respective church they represent. Unless noted otherwise, quotes cited come from the surveys.

Questions were open-ended to allow survey subjects the freedom to interact with them.

Finally, the responses given are being evaluated with these two questions in mind: "Are the experiences of the respondents consistent with what the books suggest?" and "Are there things unique to this ministry approach not captured by the literature?"

Introduction to the Churches Studied

Four of the churches—Philadelphian Community, New Creation Church, OPF, and Trinity Church—are found in the Portland, Oregon, metropolitan vicinity. The remaining two of the congregations, The Journey and Fellowship of Faith, are located in the Seattle, Washington area.

Philadelphian Community is the product of a predominantly Asian congregation joining an Anglo congregation in 2008. The Anglo church was comprised of twelve older congregants aged sixty to mid-eighties. The Asian congregation numbered between forty to fifty congregants, most with families, and the oldest congregants were in their late thirties/early forties. The two churches were both part of the Southern Baptist Convention. The older congregation owned their building, was without a pastor, and attendance was declining with the passing of its members. The younger congregation met at a local university, and their pastor was on staff part-time.

In 2000, New Creation Church formed when an African-American congregation (with a little over 200 members) joined with an Anglo congregation (of about 100). The Anglo congregation was younger, made up of people in their twenties, and had a pastor. The African-American congregation had a full-time pastor as well. The African-American congregation had their own meeting place and the Anglo congregation was renting a facility.[3] The African-American church was part of a denomination; the An-

---

3. Koe, "Races," lines 7–17, 23–24.

glo church was not. After the union of the churches, New Creation became non-denominational. New Creation kept both pastors, and the pastor of the Anglo congregation became the associate pastor of the new church.

OPF is the result of an Anglo congregation, made up of couples whose children were grown, singles and a few younger families, and a primarily Asian congregation consisting of families with school-aged children. The average age of the Asian congregation was roughly ten to fifteen years younger than that of the Anglo church. Both congregations were meeting in temporary rented locations. The Asian congregation had a pastor on staff, and the Anglo church had no staff. Both congregations were non-denominational. Before the merge, the Asian church had sixty congregants and the Anglo church had almost thirty.

Trinity Church came into being when a Korean congregation joined an Anglo congregation. Both churches had pastors and were both part of the Presbyterian Church (PCUSA). The Korean congregation, made up of younger families, was looking for a place to meet. The Anglo congregation, consisting of an older generation, had a church facility and property. The Anglo pastor was planning to retire. The Presbytery conference, aware of the circumstances for both churches, initiated the dialogue for the two congregations to come together. The Korean congregation had conducted their services in Korean, and Trinity held services in both English and Korean. The combined congregation was a little over 100 and the Korean congregation was double the size of the Anglo community. A couple years after joining together, the venture failed in 2005.[4]

The Journey was birthed in 2007[5] from an Anglo congregation with a church building, numbering at about seventy to eighty-five, inviting a larger (about 320 attendees), younger, multi-racial (mainly Asian and Anglo) congregation to join them. The younger church met in a renovated warehouse, which doubled as a public coffee shop during the week, while the Anglo congregation owned the church building next door. In addition, the multiracial church rented the Anglo congregation's church facility to augment its services and ministry to children. The Anglo church's pastor was planning for his retirement, and initiated the conversation with his leadership team to plan for the future. The churches are part of the same denomination, Evangelical Covenant.

---

4. No contact was made with any of the congregants from Trinity. The findings discussed come from conversations with one of the lead pastors who has since retired, and the pastor who replaced him. Attempts to discuss the experience with former congregants and the Korean pastor were unsuccessful.

5. Cho, "Relationship."

Churches That Became Multiracial through Merging

Fellowship of Faith is the combination of an older Anglo congregation, numbering between twenty and thirty, that had a church building and property joining together with a multiracial congregation. The multiracial congregation had a pastoral staff and the older congregation had an interim pastor. The younger, multiracial congregation of about ninety was a growing church plant established by a multiracial church in the Seattle area. They were approached by the Anglo church to join together to reach the community around the church as a multiethnic ministry. The Anglo church was part of a denomination; the multi-racial congregation was not. In 2000, when the churches joined together they became a non-denominational church.

Figure 4.1 represents the churches by characteristics of its parent congregations including year of inception. Graphically, the color of the figures indicates race (white = Anglo; gray = Asian; and black = African-American). Each small figure represents ten people. A large figure represents pastoral staff. An "R" next to the pastoral staff figure indicates the pastor is retiring. Underscored figures indicate the older congregation. The building denotes property owned by the church. If the church was multiracial it will have various hued figures (NOTE: this does NOT reflect the actual racial make-up of the parent congregation).

Figure 4.1—Churches Studied by Parent Congregation Characteristics

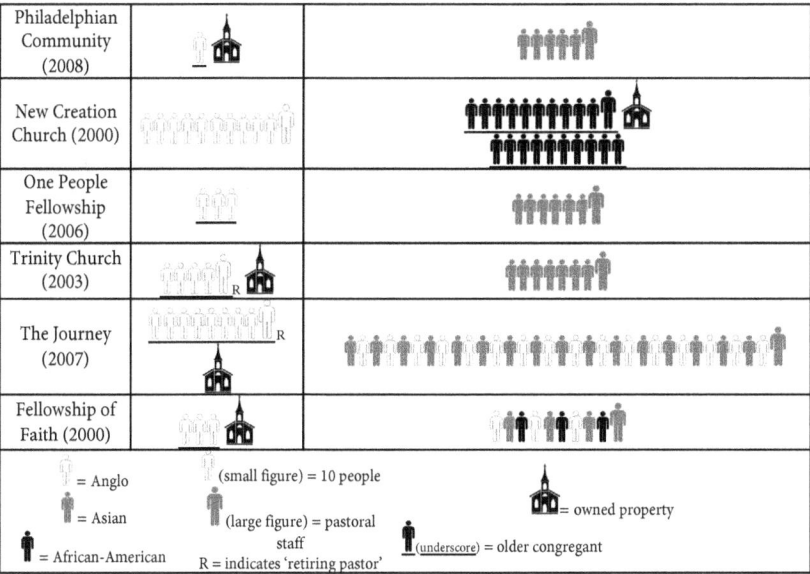

47

1 + 1 = 1

Becoming a Multiracial Ministry

Impetus for Formation

Consistent with what Emerson & Woo describe in *People of the Dream*, the formation of these multiracial congregations was prompted by "resource calculation" and/or "mission".[6] By way of the author's observation, Figure 4.2 represents the contributing factors prompting the congregations to join together.

Figure 4.2—Synopsis of Reasons for Bringing Congregations Together

Congregation	Impetus for change
Philadelphian Community	Anglo congregation needed a pastor and Asian congregation needed a place to meet
New Creation Church	Desire to further mission of both congregations
One People Fellowship	Need for change because both churches had come to a plateau, lacked critical mass and desired a bigger vision
Trinity Church	Asian congregation needed a meeting place, Anglo congregation had facility and wanted to infuse life into church
The Journey	Anglo congregation sought to be proactive in ministry and wanted to share its resources with another congregation
Fellowship of Faith	Anglo congregation was shrinking in size and wanted to share its resources with another congregation that had a vision for reaching their local community

The "impetus for change" described in the figure is the "catalyst" prompting the respective parent congregations to come together to form a new church community. These motives influenced the respective church communities to consider merging.

The motives given for creating these respective congregations are not exclusive and multiple factors were likely involved. The important common thread for all these churches is that each congregation chose to pursue

---

6. Emerson and Woo, *People*, 56. The motive for change is explored further in the next chapter.

multiracial ministry, reflecting a view counter to the status quo of racially homogeneous congregations. The creation of a multiracial ministry was deliberate. Any of the churches examined could have joined a congregation of similar race if their goal was merely to keep things going.

As a church considers why it would become a multiracial church, motive should be examined. One way to determine motive is to eliminate the reason for wanting to unite with another church by fulfilling it. For instance, if a church needed a new place to meet and this need was satisfied, would it still join another congregation?

The difference between a "motive" and a "side effect" is intent and outcome. If a side effect is eliminated, the action will still continue. However, if the main motive is eliminated, in all likelihood, the action will cease.

Pastor YQ, the Anglo pastor of Trinity Church, shares about how a mixed motive brought about the end of Trinity. He explained that an expectation some in the Korean congregation had was that the Anglo congregation would dwindle, leaving the Koreans to "inherit" a building. The Anglo congregation was aware of this hope before entering into the relationship and was fine with the potential outcome. However, the merge had a rejuvenating effect on the Anglo congregation and they eagerly welcomed their "new" brethren. Pastor YQ believes there was a "loss of face" for some members of the Korean congregation because the Anglo church embraced them in spite of the "hidden" agenda. Tensions over this and other unknown issues precipitated a conflict that led the Korean pastor and the Korean members to leave.

If the incentive to create a multiracial church is not driven by a God-conceived vision, a flawed motive can threaten the efforts of merging for a kingdom purpose.

Equipping the Congregations to be Multiracial

Changing a congregation's racial composition does not happen on a whim. In the movie *Guess Who's Coming to Dinner?*, a young, interracial couple agonizes over how to announce their engagement to their parents because they are unsure how the news will be received. This mirrors church leadership's challenge in caring for God's people. Inviting a congregation to change takes time. While most may not oppose the idea, leadership would be wise to approach the task humbly.

1 + 1 = 1

The survey responses indicate a process that took time. For some there were particular events that stood out to them as momentous, while others experienced gradual change, from conception to the decision to merge. The process involved prayer, meetings and dialogues about what the churches were getting themselves into.

How does leadership prepare their people for intercultural relationships that were previously nonexistent?

Pastor AC, an African-American and senior pastor of New Creation Church, is well-versed in racial reconciliation. As a former staff person with PromiseKeepers, one of his responsibilities was teaching others about reconciliation—talking about racialization and reconciling races (not limited to black and white) to one another. Pastor AC's experience and professional background in social work brought conversations about race into the church setting.

The other founding pastor of New Creation Church, Pastor EE, was involved with reconciliation as well. He had planted a church that was roughly 85 percent Anglo and 15 percent African-American. The individual, personal visions of the pastors shaped how they presented the merge idea to their people. Their overlapping desires for an integrated church community led them to lead their congregations together to form New Creation.

Pastor EE says it was the congregants who initiated the idea of bringing the congregations together. He had reservations about doing it and preferred partnering in ministry as separate organizations. The church he led was a younger congregation, but they were geographically and socially similar to the African-American church.

At OPF, the notion that race would be essential to creating a multiracial church was something we all accepted. Of the "founding members" of OPF, a significant portion of the Anglos had had cross-cultural experience from living overseas, doing ministry in a foreign country or as missionaries. A number of the Asians in the congregation were familiar interracial marriages, either personally or through immediate family. These prior experiences and relationships set a base of respect and value for other cultures. Inviting congregants to embrace a biblical vision of multiple races gathered together in one church was fairly simple and readily accepted, although for some, the issue of losing an ethnic-specific ministry was difficult to resolve. The complications we encountered were connected to personal, non-biblical preferences such as time and day to meet, and perceived fears of change.

In Seattle, The Journey actively talked about race issues. Some members were already having conversations about race before the merger took place. One of the parent churches sponsored a conference on race in order to introduce race and faith into the normal conversations of their church.[7]

Managing Conflict and Change

Preparing for the necessary change and inherent conflict involved in integrating racial congregations is complex. Conflict extracts costs that are emotional, spiritual, and physical. When conflict occurs across racial lines the possibility of racial bias exists, heightening tensions. The fear of being perceived "racist," as labeled by others, or self-determined by introspection, can raise additional apprehension.

Survey responses and interviews revealed that the areas of conflict span a wide range of issues, some of which were nothing more than unrealized fears. Changes in identity, leadership personnel, polity, music worship styles, ministry programs, and service order were notable problems that came up.

As might be expected in a multiracial environment, cultural expectations stemming from race also arose. When the churches were talking about joining together to form OPF, there was a concern over how conflict would be engaged and handled. Leadership recognized that because of culture, Asians and Anglos have different interpretations of confrontation, including direct and indirect communication styles.

OPF represents a circumstance where neither of the parent churches owned property. As a result, a conflict over meeting time and location arose. Schedules are typically built around meeting times (i.e., Sunday morning). If this set schedule disappears, meeting times reflect people's lifestyle choices (e.g., family activities, sports, hobbies). Leasing meeting space at another church will, in all likelihood, mean that the tenant needs to figure out when to meet other than Sunday morning. OPF discovered that some of its congregants were territorial about their preferred meeting times.

Resolving conflict can involve negotiation and compromise. To minimize the politicization of the decision, appealing to an overarching vision and core values to dictate the appropriate course of action makes conflict less personal and is driven by a greater cause than self.

---

7. Iwasaki, "Faith," July 29, 2005, lines 4–7.

Some Will Be Dissatisfied

Respondents indicated surprise at different aspects of the merge. Some were surprised at how many people left their newly merged church (more than expected). Others were surprised at the difficulty of getting people to mix between races. Some had not expected the change in music. And others had not anticipated the differences between generations.

In a telling statement concerning getting the congregation to integrate, one person responded that it was hard to "see people that were afraid and prejudiced as Christians, and they didn't want to admit it. [They] just faked it and end up leaving. [They] didn't realize it takes work to make a relationship last."

Sometimes it seemed like a collision of expectations was unavoidable. The plans and direction for the church often ran counter to a personal preference or agenda. A member of GCC Church (one of the parent congregations of OPF) wanted more time to consider joining. From their perspective, the joining was rushed, despite the two churches having spent time together to worship and fellowship for almost six months prior to deciding to come together. After the decision to join together was made, the process lasted an additional eighteen months. Similarly, another member from GCC was unhappy with the polity of the church, commenting, "I would have stayed with [GCC] if the eldership model of leadership was eliminated and leadership was shared with all who were interested so that many/all of the members' voices/concerns/ideas could be heard."

OPF discovered that attempting to please everyone can lead to disaster. The leadership of both churches tried to accommodate all congregants. In doing so the original idea to join together was abruptly called off. In this instance, there were a few congregants who did not want to change what each church had. To calm these concerns, the leadership "repackaged" the plan to sound less definitive than previously thought. To other congregants, however, especially those who were committed to the merge, this was confusing because they had the impression things were farther along than what was now being expressed. Essentially, the elders were communicating uncertainty or reluctance. A fog of confusion soon settled on both churches, leaving the enthusiastic bewildered.

In a post-mortem dialogue between the remaining elders, the events and the elders' personal motives leading to the sudden wreck were examined. The elders revisited their decision and rationale, and a few months later the plan was back on—upsetting those who hoped it would not happen. In the end, the leadership had the opportunity to upset everyone.

Look for Problems and Find Solutions

It has been said that the only time people will take advantage of a leader's "open door" policy is when they are headed out the door. This policy implies that no matter who you are, you have access to speak with the leader because they want to hear your concerns. Unfortunately, this policy can keep leadership from proactively looking for issues. Instead leaders wait for people to initiate the conversation about problems they encounter. If a person really desires information they will look for it, or, as management guru Tom Peters puts it, they "manage by walking around." Waiting for people to bring their problems to leadership might be too late.

Many of the differences and difficulties were managed by talking things through. The leadership wanted to hear people out and was empathetic to the concerns expressed. Opportunities to talk and work out issues with those who disagreed helped diffuse potential conflict points.

In Seattle, the parent churches forming the Journey had congregation-wide forums for the congregants to discuss what was going to happen. It was particularly difficult for the Anglo church with the retiring pastor and building. A number of meetings were held to help its older-generation members catch and embrace a vision that had the potential to marginalize them. They were the ones who had the most to "lose" especially because, as Pastor OY describes it, the parent church was "uniting herself with [The Journey]."[8] After a poor initial reaction ("absolutely not"), the older congregation only lost a handful of people (less than 10 percent). The key to turning things around was giving people a larger vision. As Pastor OY states,

> We were feeling pretty good about ourselves.... We need to have a larger vision.... We need to ask the questions a little differently, and the questions need to be more in line with a kingdom vision rather than a vision for IB Church. Because in thinking about those two things, they will lead you to different conclusions and different answers. This is never a choice between bad and good. It is a choice between good and good.

---

8. Pastor OY was intentionally describing a picture of marriage—something like a marriage as described in 1 Peter 3, where a wife gives herself (submits) to her husband.

> ...We started to talk about what it meant to have a "kingdom-mindedness" and to ask what's good for the kingdom of God and for the cause of Christ and the larger picture. As opposed to what's good for the survival long-term of IB Church. And that, I think, really started to open up the conversation in a lot of different ways.

Unfortunately, a limitation in the survey is knowing and understanding the success of addressing these concerns. When concerns were not resolved, what could have been done better? How and why did these efforts fail? At OPF and New Creation Church there have been hard feelings in the conflicts, and a better process for resolution would have been helpful.

Furthermore, talking things out directly tends to be a "Western"-minded solution. As Law puts it,

> In an ethnocentric way, most whites believe that inequality can be countered by simply physically including the powerless and the disadvantaged. They think that by inviting an individual representative from the powerless group to join them, they are able to redistribute power more evenly. The assumption is that everyone is equal to each other as individuals and everyone is expected to participate "fully"—meaning being able to speak for himself or herself. The truth is that not all believe they are equal to each other.
> ... Many people of color come from cultures that emphasize the collective over the individual. It is very hard for them to speak as individuals. They feel powerless without their community behind them.[9]

By way of observation, the Journey's approach to discovering people's issues in open congregational meetings was met with success because the older congregation was Anglo and the younger, multiracial congregation was made up of people who were acculturated to a "Western" approach to the discussions held. What Marti describes for Mosaic seems to apply here, "While these ethnics have not abandoned their ethnicity, they are in the process of renegotiating it toward an Americanized center."[10] For some congregations, this means a heritage-informed way of dealing with things can be diminished. Potential conflict can be resolved because there is a common, accepted format for engaging and resolving issues.

---

9. Law, *Wolf*, 34.
10. Marti, *Mosaic*, 160.

The Difficulty Is Worth It

Given the challenges of becoming multiracial and merging congregations, who in their right mind would even consider it? Since planning for conflict and change is hard enough with a church plant or a singular church ministry, what benefits could offset the pain to come from more complex ministry challenges? What makes the promise of change plus its potential conflict even worth considering?

Respondents described several joys of the process. Overwhelmingly, pursuing God's heart and seeing him show up was a strong reason for bringing churches together to form a multiracial ministry. Being able to entrust oneself to good leadership to gain these things (God's heart and witnessing His work) rounds out the top three responses for what was "easy" about bringing together congregations to create a multiracial community.

Nearly a third of the responses describe enthusiasm for being in a place where God was pleased with the outcome—bringing the churches together was a fulfillment of God's desire for both congregations. Almost a quarter of respondents stated that it was easy to be with the other congregation, spending time together in fellowship.

One person described their thoughts this way: "For me, once I truly heard the elders share their vision together from both churches and felt the Holy Spirit amongst us . . . that's all it took. There were still difficulties and snags but I caught the vision and felt the promptings the second time around."

Pastor JY of Fellowship of Faith comments that, similar to what took place with The Journey, the older congregation, welcomed the younger, multiracial church. According to Pastor YZ, the lead pastor, the only thing the multiracial congregation gave up was the name of the church. The Anglo church community wanted what the other congregation had—music, cross-cultural reach and connection, and leadership (elder rule and pastoral staff). In many respects, it was a friendly "takeover" that only required a parley over the non-negotiables. The main thing the Anglo congregation had to make a concession on was elder rule because they had a congregational polity.

The Work Can Be Heartbreaking

The joys of the ministry will help sustain leadership and anyone considering multiracial ministry through merging. But as one would expect, there are two sides to this coin. Anticipating the proverbial drop of the "other shoe," what is difficult about this ministry process?

The problems that arose were neither complex nor uncommon. They came down to human nature because change and transition can be hard. In a number of situations, what was difficult for people was the loss of relationships because of the merge. People were hurt when friends left the church because they were unhappy with the change. It seemed to communicate that church membership was more about having personal needs met rather than God's leading and relationships with others. To a much lesser extent, legal logistics and the details of anticipating, tracking and communicating the change were a burden.

Conflict and change came before and after the churches joined together. Before all the churches united with their counterparts, each reported extensive conversations (within and between congregations) that took place. To prepare their congregations for what was coming, leadership had to communicate with their people.

Sometimes People Leave Regardless of What Leadership Does

Across the board, church leadership brought the proposal before their respective congregations, shared a vision of what they believed God was calling their church to, and asked people to pray about next steps. They also conducted a number of meetings and conversations where leadership listened to the concerns of their people.

Much of what they did parallels the advice given by works described in the previous section on making two churches one. Yet, despite the efforts of both leadership and congregants, many of the churches experienced a measure of attrition because of the changes that came about.

- At Philadelphian Community, four members of the Anglo congregation left because they were there to sustain the ministry while it was just trying to stay afloat. Once the merge took place, they felt released to move to churches closer to their respective homes.

Churches That Became Multiracial through Merging

- After the churches joined together, the combined congregation of OPF, less those who left, was a little over sixty—the Asian congregation lost three families while the Anglo church lost roughly half their original number.
- For Fellowship of Faith, approximately half of the Anglo congregation left after the churches came together.
- The Journey lost about fifteen people from the Anglo congregation and less than 5 percent of the multiracial congregation left (around ten).

The issues that seem to prompt people to leave include dissatisfaction with the changes, in particular losing what the dissatisfied valued or believed they would lose—a particular ministry, relationships, and/or the way ministry was done. It is possible that people were planning to leave and the merge provided an opportunity to make a departure that actually had nothing to do with the merge.

At OPF, one family left because they had some concerns over culture. In a private conversation with the author, an individual shared that their spouse felt uncomfortable with the impending change. Apparently, there were some fears about how the culture of the church would change, and they had hesitations about interacting with people who were racially and culturally different. The concern described seemed to be over a perceived "loss of safety" because the individual was not adept at navigating intercultural social situations. They were worried about how they would be viewed, and had a self-conscious anxiety.

Upon reflection, I and other leaders could have probably done more to help this person and family work through their fears. Perhaps probing questions that might have elicited these concerns would have helped. Like the motives that help bring churches together, there was probably a complexity of motives that prompted this family to leave. Race and cultural differences combined with other concerns contributed to bringing about this family's departure.

Relationships Depend on Trust

Anticipating conflict does not mean that everything can be dealt with prior to the churches coming together. Concerns can be addressed ahead of time, but some problems are uncovered after the merge. A couple of the congregations studied experienced significant conflict after the churches joined together. The perceived loss of trust strains and breaks relationship.

Pastor YQ of Trinity Church, called their two-year venture a "grand experiment." He believes that things failed because of broken interpersonal relationships rather than a clash between cultures. Mistrust between the Korean congregation and their pastor caused a rift that could not be overcome. As people took sides within the group, relationships within this part of the congregation eroded. Despite his efforts to gain reconciliation, Pastor YQ was unable to mediate the disagreements and an exodus began for the Asians at the church.

New Creation Church experienced a significant decline when conflict arose. As Pastor EE puts it, "The first three months were great, then . . ." the "honeymoon" was over. In his estimation, things did not work out because there was conflict between the two pastors and there were cultural issues that could have been resolved had both pastors been on the same page. Instead, different expectations from white and black perspectives set the leadership against one another. Pastor AC notes that shortly after the churches joined together it grew up to 400 attendees. A few months later, disagreement amongst the leadership caused a significant rift. Nine years later, only two congregants from the original Anglo congregation remain at the church.

One Anglo respondent from New Creation explains it this way: "When it all comes down to it, the congregations did not trust each other because the leadership did not trust each other." This same person observed that "black church members did not trust [the] white church" adding that an unexpected obstacle was "[t]he pride that leadership had and could not let go of with respect to their positions. [It was] probably one of the biggest reasons for trouble because it filtered down to [the] congregation and sides were taken."

Pastor AC believes the two churches should have taken more time to get to know one another and build relationships of trust. Regarding his relationship to the other pastor, they also needed to develop their relationship. Reflecting on a scene from the movie, *A Few Good Men*, Pastor AC makes a comment on a relationship of trust between a black solider and his white squad mate. In contrast to this rapport, between himself and Pastor EE there was a problem,

> These two leaders were combating each other, the black and the white guy. Because they had not gotten to a place where they

learned to love one another and know one another, so when battle comes they didn't trust each other. So when you go through intense times as a church, if you haven't befriended, loved, and learned [about] that person, you're not going to trust them. When you hit stressful times, it's going to be tough. To get through and resolve conflict, trust provides the groundwork for the solution. This trust can be grown when there is an attitude of love and humility.[11]

Based on interviews with ministry leaders, the leadership attempted to connect with all the people who were unhappy with the merge and were planning to leave or had left. They listened to grievances, communicated concern, and gave congregants the freedom and space to leave. Some survey responses indicated that congregants were unaware of the pastoral care that had been extended to those who ended up leaving.

In the majority of self-reported departures, those who left commented that they felt the leadership drove them to leave. The relationship that had existed was broken and irreconcilable leading these individuals to leave.

As respondents reflected on why people left, there was one anomaly in responses regarding race. Some respondents observed that others, presumably the ones that left, preferred racial/ethnic-specific ministry. In one specific case the author is aware of, prior interactions created fear and distrust of a particular race. None of the self-reporting respondents indicated that race was an issue and there is no reason to doubt their answers.

It is possible that those for whom race was an issue did not participate in the survey. Race is a volatile issue and presuming racist intent is a strong assumption to make. Furthermore, because behavior and motive can be intertwined and/or indistinguishable from one another, what is observed may be fiction or reality. Speculating about "real" motives is risky, but how those who stayed felt and what they perceived is worth the attention.

Pastor EE reported that the events at New Creation were rough for him and based on subsequent experiences as a church consultant primarily involved in church plants, he suggests that merging to create a multiracial ministry is a bad idea. He recognizes it can work but it will be difficult. From his perspective, he observed, "the cultural paradigms are deeply ingrained" and will become a significant source of conflict. In his experience, he said that he has not seen any church merges work. When pressed, he thought if a merge were attempted, the congregations would need to be socially and geographically similar and would need well-defined leadership roles.

---

11. Sande, *Peacemaker*, 148.

At the end of the interview, Pastor EE reiterated that he considered merging churches across racial lines to be "like pushing water uphill," adding that it is "easier to work through the Homogeneous Unit Principle because it [merging churches between different racial groups] [will be] the hardest thing you've ever done."

Radical change is difficult. Pastor GP of OPF wisely observes: "Before you do it [join congregations together], you better count the cost if your people aren't willing to pay the price."

Merge with a Purpose

The literature observes that a multiracial church is the product of intentional ministry.[12] Likewise, a church merge requires that the congregations involved have a goal in mind because the upheavals to come need a good basis for causing the discomfort of change.[13] Merging to revitalize a ministry by creating a multiracial environment demands intentionality for both church merges and integration across racial lines.

As described by survey participants, significant reasons for embracing change (merging congregations to create a new church) were to become multiracial/multiethnic, to promote racial reconciliation, and/or to change and grow the ministry because what was currently done could not be sustained by one church. These goals were described as the basis for pursuing a new direction God was taking each church. Many felt a multiracial ministry would catalyze the merge and encourage movement in a positive direction.

In Seattle, the Anglo churches wanted to minister to a multiethnic community, and viewed the younger multiracial churches as an opportunity to do so. In Portland, the single-race congregations desired to change their ministries by crossing racial boundaries.

The pastor of Philadelphian Community noted that the Anglo church they joined with approached them. The Anglo congregation was without a pastor and wanted a younger congregation to join them because they, as a church, were literally dying. They welcomed the Asian congregation and gave them their church and received their name.

In the author's church, OPF, the joining of congregations fulfilled a dream of a couple of the key leaders. PN was a friend of the author. In the course of the relationship, they talked about the type of church they

12. Yancey, Emerson and Woo, Garces-Foley, DeYmaz, and DeYoung et al.
13. Laribee, "Factors," 80.

both longed to see come into being. In the course of a long-running conversation, they brought their respective congregations together to worship (April 2004) and, later, sponsored a community outreach event (September 2004). The success of working and relating well together led to discussions about joining the congregations (October 2004) to create a new church community (Easter 2006).

A survey respondent from One People, sums up what took place this way. Both congregations needed more "critical mass" (too small to accomplish what they hoped), and they had overlapping visions (multicultural, multigenerational) that could be realized through a merge. Personal relationship/kinship between an elder at [FBC] and an elder at [GCC] [brought the churches together]. The merge allowed both congregations to transition to a greater vision—God's desire for his people as a united Body.

The Benefit of Hindsight

In retrospect, there were a few things many felt could have been done differently. Activities that could have eased the transition, including holding moderated discussions about racial/ethnic backgrounds and perspectives, explaining how communication style is informed by racial and ethnic background, providing visual aids describing the timeline and flow of change, facilitating conversations about racially and ethnically informed values/preferences for worship (covering such things as dress, order of service, start time, emotional expression), and setting expectations of leadership (organizational roles, relationship to one another, relationship to the congregation).

Advice from survey respondents and pastors includes:

- Communicate—be clear, consistent, and frequent.
- Lead with a clear vision.
- Anticipate and prepare for change. Help congregants recognize that joining the churches together is a process requiring time, patience, work, and relational understanding.

These basic observations offer a starting place for leading churches to unite and become multiracial. This advice will be incorporated into a framework described in the next chapter.

Keep People Informed.

A consistent indicator of "success" was communication. All the respondents had something to say about communication. Good communication facilitated the transition process while poor communication held the process up.

The importance of communication was seen clearly at a personal level. From this author's perspective, the biggest weakness of the merge process for OPF was communication. The leadership did a poor job of keeping people in the loop concerning what was going on. This problem becomes increasingly evident based on some of the responses given in the survey. One response indicated its understanding of the merge was about one church saving the other from closing its doors—"[FBC] wasn't doing well and it was said by the [GCC] elders that 'they wanted what we have.' I suspect that underlying the decision to form into one church was one of the elders wanting to help [FBC] not go under, but this was not explicitly stated to the [GCC] group."

Having been part of the behind-the-scenes dialogue, this was not the intent of leadership. However, the speculation by this congregant cannot by faulted because leadership failed to provide a coherent, unified message to both congregations. What they heard created an impression. While leadership had no intention of conveying this message, it was the meaning some congregants concluded.

A significant ingredient of communication is trust. Failing to communicate clearly and with a consistent message can breed mistrust. This mistrust can be regarding ability or heart (or motive). Based on how congregants responded at OPF, it appears that those who mistrusted the motives of leadership were the ones who left. The others who trusted our motives, but could see we were doing a poor job of conveying our intent, helped us get through this problem. They did so by patiently waiting for clarification, asking incisive questions and giving gracious feedback.

By way of advice gleaned through the transition process, a congregant at One People who is by vocation a specialist at corporate communication and public relations, cautioned that when communication is poor, people will come up with their own ideas and explanations for what is going on.

Inadequately sharing information may be indicative of other problems. It may indicate uncertainty, distrust (of leadership for congregation), relational breakdown among the leadership, and/or ignorance about the importance of keeping people informed.

A key revelation for OPF was that hearing people's concerns is not the same thing as acting on them. Good communication involves listening to what congregants have on their hearts and minds. Effective leadership understands that it might not be able to keep everyone happy as it moves forward.

On the flip side, good communication engenders trust. A congregant at Philadelphian Community speaks well of the process because of how their leadership worked with them to understand what was going on. This person writes, "Make sure that you understand what is important to each congregation and coach each congregation on how to handle it. Pastor did a very good job of coaching [Philadelphian] people before the merger. Rules of engagement . . . what to do, what not to do . . . what do they like, what don't they like . . . those are good things to understand on both sides . . ." Another congregant from the church comments, "Pastor [H] & Elder [H] are great leaders, and made the transition a lot easier." Both congregations felt cared for by how their leadership ushered them through the transition process. Keeping both congregations current on the process influenced how they received the changes asked of them.

Vision and Intent are Crucial

Not only is it important to communicate, but communication must be specific. Casting a clear vision for the congregations to embrace will help them get behind the effort. Pastor JY comments on leading the churches with vision,

> Much like our children, is they have to have their own faith. To tell them first, that God says it in the Bible, this is the way. Your people have to really believe it first. It's supposed to be multiethnic. And I go back to Acts 13 and I say, "Well, this is what it is supposed to look like." They have to believe that first. Not just because mommy or daddy said it. Somewhere along the line your kids are going to have to have [their] own faith. I think this is where you have to open it up first. They have to believe in the vision first. You have to plant it. You have to teach it. And it may take some time for them to get used to it.

Pastor YZ concurs, remarking, "To merge a church with that goal, multiethnicity in mind, you have to be able to set up a process so that it will happen. I went to a church a long time ago with the possibilities of doing something with them. They had that value statement of being multiethnic. And I asked, 'Is that happening?' And they said, 'No.' And I said, 'How long has that statement been up there?' It had been up there for years . . . in that process, there has to be some kind of intentionality."

Being able to articulate a vision that captures the heart of the people—especially decision-makers—can be a turning point, too. Pastor OY recalls a significant moment in the merger consideration process, revealing,

> One evening there was a breakthrough. This is now, time-wise, early 2007. I kept using the expression that seemed to stumble people "of giving ourselves to The Journey."
>
> . . . [O]ne of the leadership team members said (stuttering), "What?! Did I hear you say you want to give all of this, everything?"
>
> I said, "That's right, that's right. That's pretty much it." I said, "You know, because if you have a kingdom-mindedness, I don't care whether the name of this church is [———]. Isn't the important thing that we want to have a positive influence and presence in this community and beyond for many years to come? Can we not risk ourselves to do that as the people of EC Church years ago risked themselves? They did the same thing." And one of the members who was so most vehemently objecting was a part of that. I said, "John, you were part of that. You were in, your what, twenties then?"
>
> . . . [T]hen, one of the other leadership team members who is 40-ish said, "This is really giving ourselves to the next generation, isn't it?"
>
> I said, "Bingo!"
>
> Once the leadership team at IB Church was able to grasp the weight of what Pastor OY was asking them to accept, the process accelerated forward.

Help People Prepare for Change

Pastor OY pointed out how important it was for the church to help people prepare and get acclimated to the changes. "In the transition plan we were very transparent. We said, 'There are going to be some more painful changes. The pews are going to have to go.' That was all identified. There [was nothing too small]. Once we voted, 'yes,' we tried to be as open and honest as we could, as respectful as we could."

Their transition plan dealt with everything they could think of. It included leadership changes (board representation) and agreed-upon position and responsibility changes. The plan also reported financial giving of pastoral staff to the church, staff integration into one team, establishment of the transition care team (including such things as font size on bulletin and volume levels out of consideration for older members) and extra visibility of the outgoing leadership.

The Journey was proactive about listening to their people. Pastor OY shared, "We promised people that all of their issues and concerns would be heard by the elder board. There was nothing considered too frivolous or stupid or silly. It would all be heard. We did not guarantee that there would be changes implemented as a result."

Allow Adequate Time for Change

The process of bringing the congregations together varies—from the time the leadership of both congregations sat down together to the combining of congregations and assets. For five of the churches, the process ranged from three to six months.[14]

Based on the interviews with pastors, the speed of the merge process was facilitated by the congregations' perceived needs (sense of urgency driven by needing a meeting place or for pastoral care) and/or a readiness to act on God's leading.

The process of change for OPF took longer because issues of congregational identity were harder to work through. For the Asian congregation, they had to change their focus of ministering predominantly to Asians. The Anglo congregation was contending with a different identity issue connected to their philosophy of ministry. Ultimately, the congregations that made up OPF did not lose what they feared (relational connection, ethnic identity, and evangelistic opportunities). Under-communication made the process longer than probably necessary.

The problems churches faced seemed to be more issues of perception and fear of an imagined future than actual substance. Change takes time because people need to come to terms with their objections and motives. Leadership is responsible for helping people work through the process, and it can be a hard journey.

---

14. The average was five months, not including OPF.

Here is one exercise for identifying issues/motives hindering a church merge. The answers to these questions might reveal what people are struggling with. If one of the churches suddenly closed its doors and its congregation all joined the other church, would there be any objections? Why not? Would the new members be allowed to participate in helping lead the church? Could they share in shaping how ministry is done at this church?

There is ample theological and literary support for multiracial congregations and church mergers. Both ministry approaches bring congregations change and conflict, and the task is to lead churches through instability to create a healthy, lasting ministry. Some churches have attempted to do both at the same time—become multiracial by merging congregations. This work has proven to be difficult because of the changes involved and the demands it makes on leadership and congregants.

5

A New Philosophy

IN THE STAGE MUSICAL, *You're a Good Man Charlie Brown*, Charlie Brown's sister, Sally, is trying to figure out how to deal with life in response to an unexpected event. Her song reflects a new, simple philosophical one-line approach to managing future problems. If only life were so free and easy.

A church thinking about joining their congregation with a racially distinct congregation is faced with a significant paradigm shift that is neither simple nor easy. Philosophically, they enter unfamiliar territory because few have taken this ministry approach.

The Church in the United States faces a couple of issues that can affect how ministry is done—a changing racial population and a growing theological awareness that racial homogeneity is not God's eternal intent for his people. How will the church change from the prevailing model of racially homogeneous congregations?

The challenge of creating a multiracial congregation from monoracial churches is significant. Combining the task of creating a new Body by merging with starting a racially integrated ministry will multiply the potential for stress and is a certain invitation to conflict. Yet, the opportunity to advance and magnify the reputation of Christ by pursuing this ministry approach is worth the investment. Besides identifying the biblical soundness and challenges of this venture, this book offers suggestions that can facilitate success. In this chapter, the author will consider key observations gleaned from churches in the midst of this work and ministry experience that addresses the dynamics encountered in the effort.

1+1=1

A Theological View on Forming Multiracial Congregations through Mergers

There is a solid biblical basis for a multiracial church and significant theological justification for merging congregations, but is there anything that supports both at the same time?

Unfortunately, the Bible says nothing about church merges that lead to multiracial congregations. Initial objections dismissing this ministry approach are primarily based on pragmatism. Valid concerns assert that the time and cost (e.g., financial, emotional, mental, physical, etc.) required in building such a church could be better spent. Given the difficulty of the work, the resources poured into this work could be used for something more profitable. These practical arguments raise a fair point, but it would be wise to understand God's heart on the subject rather than assuming the answer is "obvious."

This author believes that in creating a multiracial church from single race congregations we learn about and express God's heart concerning race, his people, and reconciliation. Moreover, unique to the nature of this ministry, one can experience the challenges of interpersonal relationships and dependence on God to overcome preconceived notions about ministry.

Certainly, not everyone is called to do ministry in this fashion and it is not without reason that some question the efficacy of such an undertaking. Apart from the time and material resource, there can be heart-rending conflict. The potential for the reputation of Christ to be harmed by people leaving the church out of anger or discouragement is real.

The Cost of this Kingdom Venture

> 3 Then Mary took about a pint of pure nard, an expensive perfume; she poured it on Jesus' feet and wiped his feet with her hair. And the house was filled with the fragrance of the perfume. 4 But one of his disciples, Judas Iscariot, who was later to betray him, objected, 5 "Why wasn't this perfume sold and the money given to the poor? It was worth a year's wages." (John 12:3–5, NIV)

Being called to this ministry approach makes it easier to persevere through what will come. Creating multiracial churches by merging congregations can have significant kingdom impact. But what does it cost congregations

A New Philosophy

to do this? Jesus asks his people to count the cost of following him.[1] Yet, how do we balance what we believe to be cost-prohibitive against God's view of cost? If we count the cost and believe the expense of merging to create multiracial churches is not worth it, can we dismiss the approach?

In response to the question, "Would you do it again?," Pastor EE says he would not. His reasons come down to the difficulty of the work and the number of believers he saw hurt in the process when he attempted it. Furthermore, he believes it is more effective for "Jew to minister to Jew, and for Gentile to reach out to Gentile." Of the large number of church consults he's done, he says he has never seen or experienced a healthy congregation that was the result of a merge. It is his opinion that a church plant is a much better way to go because it is a better use of time and money, and a proven approach for growing the Body of Christ.

In Mal 1:8–14, God is infuriated with how his people, the nation of Israel, are treating him. The text describes Israel's offense[2] and people's disrespect of God. But why did Israel do this? Perhaps they were just going through the motions of ritual and tradition. As far as they were concerned, anything you threw on the altar was good enough. Yet, God asked for the best quality of harvest and animals. From their perspective, they believed wasting good animals for sacrifice made little sense if lesser quality beasts could suffice.

From a human perspective, it makes little sense for God to ask us to give him the best, the most valuable of our possessions, only to destroy them on an altar as an act of worship. We might think, "If God is not going to do anything more than destruction, we can come up with something more productive." This type of waste seems ludicrous and akin to taking a $100 bill and burning it up with a match.[3] Yet God has asked, and continues to ask, his people to make such a decision. The appearance of waste does not bother God because, regardless of what we think, it serves his purpose. This is a lesson with timeless implications—God may be asking us to sacrifice our most valued assets (i.e., time, effort, material possessions, and health). Depending on our attachment to these things, he may be asking us to release our "idols."

With this in mind, time, finances and effort are a questionable basis for determining whether or not a multiracial church is worth pursuing.

---

1. Luke 14:26–28.
2. They offered God inferior, defiled animals for sacrifice in violation of Lev 22:17–25.
3. Or using perfume to anoint feet, John 12:3–5.

While it may seem to us that a multiracial church is too expensive when the resources could be used for a "more fruitful" harvest, this might miss the bigger picture. God's goals and plans are more ambitious than ours, and he invites us to do things from his perspective.[4]

Admitting that we are not cut out for the work of multiracial ministry is more honest than suggesting there are better things we can do with our time. What is the difference? One viewpoint understands that God issues the call and invites us to his work. The other presupposes that we know how to best spend what God has given to us, and we should not "waste" these resources.

Theologian Charles Van Engen offers another way for evaluating multiracial ministry starts:

> Here is the issue. These [models for multicultural church planting] should not be evaluated only on the basis of whether they grow numerically, nor only on whether they "work" in terms of reducing cultural conflict and preserving the cohesion of groups. They should not even be evaluated on whether they are well received by the people or groups in a particular context. I believe the primary criterion on which models should be evaluated is the extent to which they are able to preserve a contextually appropriate balance between the UNIVERSALITY and the PARTICULARITY of the Church. We should seek to avoid both cultural blindness nor cultural imposition. Thus, given a particular missional context, particular styles of leadership, specific cultural emphases, and concrete changes occurring over time, the models that best seem to foster a complementarity of universality and particularity should be the ones we encourage. In other words, we should seek to balance the "multi" aspects with the "ethnicity" factors.[5]

Van Engen affirms and celebrates differences, but ethnicity should not be the basis of unity in the church. While the church seeks to include and respect the particularities of race and ethnicity, the universal message of the gospel is central for unity. The message of the gospel "must complement rather than eclipse the marvelous richness of ethnic diversity which can be fostered in multi-ethnic congregations."[6] Both are needed in the church. When expedience influences how churches are established, the chance of missing out on God's invitation to partake in his work increases.

4. Isa 55:8–9.
5. Van Engen, " Church for Everyone?," 36.
6. Ibid., 37.

Pragmatism rationalizing this ministry work is inadequate, too. Merging congregations because it makes sense (e.g., putting a dying congregation with a building together with a younger congregation that has financial resources and energy) is flawed and may have the wrong motivation behind it.

The Benefit of this Kingdom Venture

All this is from God, who reconciled us to himself through Christ and gave us the ministry of reconciliation (2 Cor 5:18, NIV)

In the context of multiracial churches, congregations that join together reflect the reconciliation Paul describes in 2 Cor 5. Uniting local bodies of Christ can showcase the reconciliation of people to God, and to one another. Merging congregations is not just about sharing the same space because, as Garces-Foley states, "it is quite possible for an institution to be inhabited by people of diverse ethnic identities without engendering any substantial crossing of ethnic boundaries or creating a community of equals. The mere presence of diversity, after all, does not necessarily lead to integration, substantial cross-cultural interaction, racial reconciliation, celebration of differences, or ethnic inclusion in any meaningful sense."[7] Reconciliation within the Body of Christ involves integration and mutual relationship.

Bringing congregations together can lead to renewal—churches create a more complete local body by adding "body parts" that were missing. The "missing" gifts given for the good of the Body, in 1 Cor 12 may be discovered anew when assemblies are combined. While these spiritual gifts may already be present within a given body, their expression may be different because of race, ethnicity, and culture.

Commenting on being the Body of Christ made one by the Spirit, Volf notes this about 1 Cor 12, "baptism into Christ creates a people as the differentiated body of Christ. Bodily inscribed differences are brought together, not removed. The body of Christ lives as a complex interplay of differentiated bodies—Jewish and Gentile, female and male, slave and free —of those who have partaken of Christ's self-sacrifice. The Pauline move is not from the particularity of the Body to the universality of the Spirit, but from separated bodies to the community of interrelated bodies—the one

---

7. Garces-Foley, *Crossing*, 82.

Body in the Spirit with many discrete members."[8] The Body of Christ is intended by God to be diverse, united, and integrated.

Looking further at this text, consider for a moment, how one expresses a particular gift will be shaped by the lens of culture. While obvious, this is an overlooked characteristic of spiritual gifts. This is significant because our understanding and appreciation of a spiritual gift may be incomplete if all we know is informed by a narrow band of life's experience. For instance, how a Sudanese exercises the spiritual gift of helps[9] might be different from a Brazilian, Swede, Indonesian, or Arab. Therefore, what the Body experiences when the gift is expressed can reveal something we would miss when we are segregated.

At a deeper level, how each person encounters Christ, the ultimate grace gift, is necessary for the building and strengthening of the Body.[10] Specifically, where Jesus meets each of us, is affected by a myriad of factors—race, socioeconomics, class, education, parents, geography, time, technology, physical abilities and limitations, cultural norms and mores, etc. The uniqueness of our life experiences and brokenness shape how we understand Christ and what he offers. A person's individual encounter and story with God is unique and exceptional. We need these perspectives to appreciate the richness and infinite depth of God, Father, Son, and Spirit.

Elmer gives an example of how differences are important to the Body. He points out that Western and non-Western styles of communication are distinct. "Directness in language implies that one can speak to a problem without offending the person. Western culture tends to separate the person from the problem, the person from the action or the person from the idea."[11] Because a non-Western worldview worries about shaming an individual when providing help, then how non-Westerners express consideration and care will differ from the Western expression.

Like Mosaic Church in Los Angeles, OPF wanted people to be drawn to Christ with our church's core values as the means of affinity. Yet, almost three years later, the church is revisiting this idea because we have discovered weaknesses in how we attempt to connect with the Hispanic and African-American communities. The reason we did not see this as an

---

8. Volf, *Exclusion*, 48.

9. 1 Cor 12:28.

10. Eph 4:7–16. In this author's opinion, the testimony of an individual's own salvation story is an overlooked gift.

11. Elmer, *Conflict*, 49.

A New Philosophy

immediate problem to address is because we started our ministry with an "ethnic transcendence" perspective. Because of competing priorities, we lacked an urgency to question this approach to diversification.

Over time, we have come to realize the value of meeting Jesus in the context of how people have encountered him—through the lens of their life's experience. Some of our congregants have come out of addiction backgrounds. Their personal stories about how Christ rescued them are informed by their brokenness.[12] Likewise, one's upbringing as informed by race or ethnicity prescribes a dimension to one's salvation story that can be minimized by ethnic transcendence.[13] We are still in the process of learning how to cross race boundaries to go beyond our Asian/Anglo mix.

Over fifty years ago, Willem Visser t'Hooft observed, "The Christian sees distinctions of race as part of God's purpose to enrich mankind with a diversity of gifts. Against racial pride or race antagonism the church must set its face implacably as rebellion against God. Especially in its own life and worship there can be no place for barriers because of race or colour."[14] A multiracial congregation communicates God's desire for reconciliation and unity across the racial divide.

A weakness, perhaps failure, of the HUP is that it is based on comfort, when the cross calls us to expect an uncomfortable life. As Miroslav Volf points out, "To claim the comfort of the Crucified while rejecting his way is to advocate not only cheap grace but a deceitful ideology."[15]

The church will not make sense to the world around it. Paul reminds believers:

> **18** *For the word of the cross is folly to those who are perishing, but to us who are being saved it is the power of God.* **19** *For it is written, "I will destroy the wisdom of the wise, and the discernment of the discerning I will thwart."* **20** *Where is the one who is wise? Where is the scribe? Where is the debater of this age? Has not God made foolish the wisdom of the world?* **21** *For since, in the wisdom of*

---

12. People with addictions are not necessarily different from those without "addictive" behaviors because everyone has areas in which we struggle. At OPF, we regularly share about how God meets us in areas of weakness including pride, alcohol, drugs, infidelity, pornography, and control.

13. A "transcendence" approach can miss the significance of meeting Jesus where we are at as determined by such things as social class, economic status, education, gender, religion, or dysfunction.

14. Visser t'Hooft, *Racial Problem*, 48.

15. Volf, *Exclusion*, 24.

> *God, the world did not know God through wisdom, it pleased God through the folly of what we preach to save those who believe.* (1 Cor 1:18–21, ESV)

This truth refers to believing in the crucified Christ (verse 23). By extension, it can include the consequences of following Jesus because of his crucifixion and resurrection. Living by our convictions, as Christians, is supposed to result in a transformed lifestyle. The challenges and difficulties of a multiracial church and church merge might seem foolish and not make much sense to other believers.

Bringing churches together to create a new congregation is in line with the heart of God. Ministering across racial boundaries can highlight the message of unity, forgiveness, and reconciliation.

6

Key Challenges of Forming Multiracial Congregations through Mergers

BASED ON THE EXPERIENCES of the churches interviewed, as well as primary and secondary sources, I believe the following are important issues to be aware of when creating a multiracial congregation by joining congregations together. The process of making it work has three challenges to address: relational, leadership, and integration.

The Relational Challenge of Multiracial Churches

Creating a multiracial congregation from monoracial assemblies is like a marriage. There is an element of give and take in the new union occurring both before and after the wedding. There will be rough spots as the newlyweds learn things about one another. There are days when they might wonder, "What have I gotten myself into?" Leaders and congregants will probably encounter the same thing when the honeymoon is over.

The following are some things churches should be aware of as they consider the consolidation of their ministries.

People Tend to Associate with Those Most Like Them

If a homogeneous church community is characterized by people who prefer the company of those most like them because it minimizes conflict, than a heterogeneous church community might be described as people who, with tongue firmly planted in cheek, are looking for a fight. To develop a racially diverse church environment, congregants have to work through their differences, especially if they plan to keep their church from reverting to homogeneity.

It can be easy to fall back into familiar habits and have relationships with people who are racially similar and/or with whom there is already a relationship. It takes effort to break this relational inertia.

There are sensible explanations for why congregants prefer people who are racially similar. In a news article, Paul DeYoung explains that blacks he spoke with wanted a racial timeout. Therefore, a racially homogeneous church becomes a place of refuge.[1] In some instances, the church is a means for preserving ethnic culture and, "can easily assume the role as the protector of ethnic identity, it is recognized as a promoter of social integration, it serves as a validation for ethnic values and customs, it gives ethnic members a place to have their individual dignity affirmed when they may be considered as lower in status by non-members, it promotes a conservatism that is conducive for ethnic preservation, and it condones deliberate social exclusiveness from outsiders."[2]

The church, through multiracial congregations, is a countercultural picture of human relationships. Commenting about the importance of separating itself from the world around it, Volf charges, "Unaware that our culture has subverted our faith, we lose a place from which to judge our own culture. In order to keep our allegiance to Jesus Christ pure, we need to nurture commitment to the multicultural community of Christian churches. We need to see ourselves and our own understanding of God's future with the eyes of Christians from other cultures, listen to voices of Christians from other cultures so as to make sure that the voice of our culture has not drowned out the voice of Jesus Christ, 'the one Word of God.'"[3] A multiracial church can catch the attention of people accustomed to voluntary segregation.

Not only can the church demonstrate something different, it can herald change to be followed. Angrosino asserts,

> The church is thus gifted in being a recognized and honored vehicle for the transmission of values that form a common ground for most of the disparate elements that make up the patchwork of American cultural diversity.

1. Blake, "Segregated," lines 19–20.
2. Fong, *Racial Equality*, 152–53.
3. Volf, *Exclusion*, 53–54.

Key Challenges of Forming Multiracial Congregations through Mergers

> Religion, in general, and Christianity in America, in particular, have played another role in the process of normative reinforcement to the extent that they have occasionally pushed general norms a bit further than society has initially been willing to embrace.
>
> . . . But the fact that the moral dimensions of the debate have been articulated through a Christian conscience indicates that just as the churches have a role in reinforcing norms already established and widely accepted, so they have a role in expanding our awareness of the moral dimensions of our decisions. It is precisely the culturally diverse society that invites Christians to this sort of positive witness, since relatively few other respectable institutions that can serve that function.[4]

The example of intercultural relationships in the church can be like a city on a hill.[5]

Some want to be with those who are different

The challenge of racial homogeneity may be easier to overcome than expected. There are indications that the differences between races may be catalytic to growing a church rather than causing it to not form or fall apart. According to the Hartford Institute for Religion Research Faith Communities Today 2005 study, multiracial congregations are growing. It notes that "congregations that are composed of two or more racial/ethnic groups are most likely to have experienced strong growth in worship attendance. Least likely to grow rapidly are predominantly white, non-Hispanic congregations. Among these congregations, only 31% experienced the highest level of growth from 2000 to 2005. Not only is the Anglo majority a shrinking proportion of the American population, but racial/ethnic minority churches and multi-racial/ethnic churches tend to be newer and to have more dynamic, exciting, and inspirational worship services."[6] The study associates growth with excitement, innovation and recruitment.

Unfortunately, this gives the impression that multiracial ministry is more a fad or marketing gimmick than an eternal kingdom quality. The Hartford study seems to suggest that multiracial congregations are perceived as cutting-edge, implying that its unusual nature creates a "cool"

---

4. Angrosino, *Talking*, 47–48.
5. Matt 5:14.
6. Hadaway, *FACTs*, 3.

factor that makes it trendy and fashionable. Pastor AC encountered a situation mirroring the study's observation: "Someone said to me, 'I like coming to [New Creation], it's kind of like a novelty.' Do people think this is something like a little fad, it's not going to stick around? Or, we have people just [. . .] do things for just a short period time!? No! No, this is going to be the church of Christ! That just blew me away. How in the world could a person think that?! Because it looks new and everything, it becomes not real?! It blew me away! That just stuck in my craw! I mean . . . C'mon, how could they think that?!"

Perhaps people are now catching up with what has always been "in." The perceived countercultural vibrancy of multiracial ministry may be the result of comparing it to an "abnormal" construct resulting from people's desire to be "safe." Maybe racially homogeneous congregations are actually aberrations of what is normative in the kingdom scheme.[7]

The growth of multiracial and multiethnic ministries may also be the result of a simpler, overlooked dynamic—second and third generation ethnics accustomed to racial diversity and integration. Marti observes, "Churches may effectively accomplish diversification by focusing on the acculturated children and grandchildren of immigrants. If white-dominant churches keep up with popular culture, second- and third-generation immigrants will be more able to access a spirituality based on a culture they have come to understand."[8] He continues,

> The experience of Mosaic suggests that truly multiethnic congregations are more likely to emerge from predominantly Caucasian churches if, instead of reaching out to a culture they have never known, they catch up to the culture of which they are already members.
>
> . . . Caucasian pastors may diversify their churches more quickly if they are willing to move their churches into contemporary culture, which is becoming increasingly globalized, and mobilize themselves not so much to reach first-generation immigrants, who are isolated from the churches' patterns of life, but their children and grandchildren, who are already in mainstream America's schools, offices, and grocery stores.[9]

---

7. This does not diminish or eliminate the necessity of homogeneous congregations. They are very important to immigrant/language-specific congregations. In some cases, homogeneous churches may have outlived their purpose and hold the church back from integration.

8. Marti, *Mosaic*, 188.

9. Ibid.

In this light, Marti describes a population at large that is shifting away from race and ethnicity as a common tie around which people associate. Instead, a shared, socially-driven culture brings people together.

Popular culture portrays an integrated, multiracial society as ideal, even normative. As a pervasive message and aspiration, it is not unreasonable to anticipate that it will be a growing expectation, especially with younger generations, as the Hartford study shows. If God designed the church to reflect racial integration, why is the church following society when it should be leading?

Scripture clearly shows that racially integrated congregations are expected. If the church follows culture, as it has in the past, it will gradually move toward racially integrated church communities. If it does so, it will do it as a laggard. Instead, the church should be leading the way and inviting society to follow its example.

Andy Crouch's book, *Culture Making*, describes how the church can be a significant force in altering the world we live in. He writes, "Culture—making something of the world, moving the horizons of possibility and impossibility—is what human beings do and are meant to do. Transformed culture is at the heart of God's mission in the world, and it is the call of God's redeemed people."[10] Summing up our call as those who invite others to the Culture of Christ, Crouch encouragingly notes, "we are made to change the world. We are made to do so at small scales and (occasionally, and probably not as often as we think, hope or expect) at large scales. We are culture makers."[11]

Hadaway points out that people are looking for a multiracial/multicultural church community. Marti and Crouch see a church that can lead or follow society into cross-cultural relationships. Regardless of what it does, the opportunity for the church in the United States is significant. Adam Edgerly, Site Pastor of NewSong Los Angeles Covenant Church, sees a promising opening for the Body of Christ: "I think there is an emerging culture in our society that wants to be multicultural, a segment of society where it is fashionable. People are recognizing how beneficial and fun it is to be with peoples of diverse backgrounds. The church is lagging behind contemporary society on this, and we are more segregated than the outer

---

10. Crouch, *Culture Making*, 189.
11. Ibid., 200.

society and have not caught on as to how great being with diverse cultures can be."[12]

We, through the Spirit's work in us, can change. Our destiny is to be transformed into the likeness of Jesus.[13] This process of transformation, invites those who do not know God to also change.[14]

Interracial Relationships Are Hard Work

Church consultant Lyle E. Schaller, in his reflections on ministry, asserts that diversity in the church is a lot harder to cultivate and maintain than most expect. He candidly notes his observations on diversity in congregational life:

> First, the greater the degree of diversity, the greater the stress on the minister. Second, the greater the emphasis on the religious aspects of life, the easier it is to accommodate diversity, while the greater the emphasis on interpersonal relationships, the more difficult it is to retain that high level of diversity. Third, the greater the diversity among the members, the more important the need to enhance the group life of the congregation so everyone who feels that need can find a homogeneous unit group or "home" within that diversity. In other words, diversity usually produces complexity. Those who want life to be simple and easy to understand and prefer the uncomplicated tend to resist expanding the group life in order to accommodate that diversity.
>
> Fourth, the greater the degree of diversity, the more critical the personality of the pastor as a central cohesive and unifying force. Fifth, the greater the diversity, the more disruptive changes in staff leadership tend to be, so longer pastorates should be part of a strategy for enhancing diversity. Sixth, the greater the degree of diversity, the more essential a consistent "affirm and build" style of leadership by the pastor. Finally, the greater the degree of diversity among the members, the more likely it will be wise to expect that one result will be a broad and highly varied program with an extremely complex schedule and an exceptionally redundant system of internal communication.[15]

12. Kinoshita, "Heaven," *Prism*, 2006, 11.
13. 2 Cor 3:18.
14. 2 Cor 5.
15. Schaller, *Reflections*, 21–22.

Schaller's concern is that it is difficult for one minister to be skilled enough to handle all their basic responsibilities capably. The nuance of diversity compounds the challenge.

Priest and Priest describe the breakdown of an attempted union between an African-American congregation, Fellowship Church, and an Anglo congregation, Community Church, in South Carolina. The merge attempt fell apart because they were unable to settle their differences. The churches had distinct expectations and the collision of these disparate views caused problems. Talking about worship at an individual level, Priest and Priest prophetically speak to the congregations' issues, "In our case study, the churches did not differ significantly in religious belief. But they did differ in historically shaped worship practices. When one aligns one's body with others in ritual, or "tunes" to another to coproduce music mutually assessed as "beautiful," one builds solidarity. But when one expects others to align, to harmonize, and they do not, this produces profound disalignment."[16] While Priest and Priest focus on the discordant music worship styles of these two churches, they also uncover underlying factors contributing to the failed attempt.

Priest and Priest observe that values informed by cultural background influenced expectations of what was spiritual and unspiritual. They write,

> Different practices, of course, reflected different ideals—and conflicting ideals resulted in various forms of assessment and judgment. There was a clear pattern at Fellowship of leadership being based on giftedness, experience, and age, while at Community it rested on formal credentials, professional training, and technical expertise. Elders and pastor at Community were young and seminary trained.
>
> ... In their [Fellowship's] view, one was not musical, however proficient one might be at playing piano, if one could only follow the sheet of music, and could not compose or play by ear. A reference to voice lessons elicited chuckles from Fellowship members, with the lead singer commenting that singing was "either something you've got or you haven't got." Deacon Ames, Mother Ames, Sister Page, and others lost standing in part because key decision makers (Bill and Pastor Smith) were from the other church and operated out of different criteria of judgment.[17]

---

16. Priest and Priest, "Divergent Worship," 285.
17. Ibid., 282–83.

1 + 1 = 1

Expectations and racial differences

A significant challenge for multiracial ministries is the fundamental differences that result from life experience. Because the African-American experience is different from other racial groups, such as those of Asians and Hispanics, integration is more difficult.[18] Marti writes, "African Americans in the United States have their own distinct American culture separate from white American culture (and from every immigrant culture coming into the United States). African Americans attempting to assimilate into a white culture make a cultural leap."[19]

Emerson explains this with more depth, describing the existence and significance of two indigenous American cultures—black and white.[20] "Most Americans seem unaware that there are two indigenous American cultures. Non-blacks especially view white culture as American, and black culture as a subculture or simply as the culture of blacks."[21] Not understanding this cultural nuance can inhibit establishing a truly integrated multiracial body.

For a multiracial ministry to flourish, recognizing and valuing both cultures will facilitate intercultural relationships. Seeing them as contributors to the Body of Christ as described in 1 Cor 12 puts the differences in a light that instills appreciation. Making room for leaders from different cultural contexts distributes power and gives people representation in the ministry, akin to Acts 5 and the Hellenist Jews.

David Anderson observes, "Black and white churches have traditionally been at opposite poles politically and culturally. Their ability to trust one another is very low."[22]

One of the challenges New Creation Church leadership faced dealt with cultural preferences informed by race. This racial divide points to the importance of dealing in reality and working through issues, especially those concerning cultural preferences.

In what he calls, "the white gloves incident", Pastor EE recalled a stir that arose between the older African-Americans and the younger Anglos. He described a tradition of the older generation wearing white gloves

---

18. Marti, *Mosaic*, 189.
19. Ibid., 189.
20. Emerson and Woo, *People*, 134–41.
21. Ibid., 139.
22. Anderson, *Multicultural*, 46.

along with formal attire (suits) when greeting people at the entrance of the church. The younger people were partial to shorts and flip-flops. The older congregants were upset by the informal dress because they perceived it as disrespect for God. After a sit-down discussion involving leadership, the African-American members, as Pastor EE puts it, "capitulated" on the issue with the younger members dressing up a little more to show respect.

At OPF, we found that differences in how Asians and Anglos communicate can lead to misunderstanding. On one such occasion, the leadership was discussing how we would address a need that had arisen. An Asian congregant shared their situation, and the leadership proceeded to sort out its plan of action. In the course of discussion, two leaders (both Anglo) expressed frustration about why the person was not more direct and seemed to them this was passive-aggressive behavior. The others (two Asians and one Anglo) explained that this person was entrusting themselves to us to make the "right" decision. To say more than necessary would cause a "loss of face." Our "responsibility," as leaders, was to look out for this person's "best interest" and "create" a viable solution.

Within a frame shaped by culture, the person wanting help was submitting themselves to the leadership of the church. Their conduct had biblical precedence, as per Heb 13:17. Incorrect assumptions could have led to a false perception about this individual and created a problem larger than what we started with.

An environment that creates space for people to manage their cultural baggage and grow through the process can turn cultural collisions into lessons about relationship. Malcolm Gladwell remarks that cultural communication barriers can be difficult to breach, but it is necessary to do so because of their potential impact. Summarizing how culture created an unhealthy submission to authority and led to airplane crashes that could have been avoided, Gladwell opines, "Why are we so squeamish? Why is the fact that each of us comes from a culture with its own distinctive mix of strengths and weaknesses, tendencies and predispositions, so difficult to acknowledge? Who we are cannot be separated from where we're from—and when we ignore that fact, planes crash."[23] A safe environment to have frank conversations is needed in order to work through the issues and concerns congregants will bring to the table.

A safe environment includes a willingness to enter into the hard conversations. Christerson, Edwards, and Emerson point out an emotionally

---

23. Gladwell, *Outliers*, 221.

charged subject that some might rather avoid because it is an uncomfortable place to go.

> Whites are accustomed to being in control in social contexts. Their norms and values are in most cases accepted without challenge. These characteristics afford whites far greater opportunity relative to racial minorities. . . .
>
> However, whites are not necessarily aware of their privileged status as the dominant racial group, nor are they aware of how their own actions perpetuate it. . . . Unless whites are conscious of the status and privileges afforded them through whiteness, and unless they act to dismantle the structure that sustains that privilege, they will by default reproduce the racialized social order.[24]

Tackling an issue such as white privilege and racialization is going to invite conflict. But it also can bring about significant growth in faith and interpersonal relationships.

Garces-Foley offers an insightful reflection:

> [the multiethnic church] turns on its head the idea that church is supposed to be a place of familiarity and comfort. The theology of discomfort reframes the costs of the multiethnic church in light of the Gospel, imbuing even minor inconveniences with theological significance. The multiethnic church member is expected to embrace difference and to find religious growth in cross-cultural encounters, which are fraught with ambiguity and discomfort. In other words, the experience of discomfort becomes a primary source of faith development.[25]

A willingness to step into a dialogue that puts relationships on the line and makes people vulnerable can strengthen the relationships at church. "Interracial relationships require give and take, leadership and followership, talking and listening, conflict and resolution. At times there may be the discomfort of stepping on each other's toes."[26]

---

24. Christerson et al., *Against*, 172.
25. Garces-Foley, *Crossing*, 133.
26. Anderson, *Multicultural*, 52.

Key Challenges of Forming Multiracial Congregations through Mergers

Assimilation hinders a relationship of equals

It is important for a multiracial environment to provide opportunities for believers to express their faith, as informed by their racial heritage and perspective. Differences shaped by race and ethnicity influence one's encounter with God. In turn, these encounters reveal facets of God that would otherwise be "undiscovered" in a homogeneous congregation. These facets are meant to help other believers grow in their faith and understanding of God.

Assimilation into a monoracial/mono-cultural ministry will make a multiracial environment difficult to create. As previously noted, the presence of diversity does not mean there is integration. Likewise, diversity does not suggest that all cultural views (from a racial context) are equally accepted.

Randy Woodley, a Native American, comments on an all too common application of assimilation: "The official policy of most churches, for example, says that everyone is welcome. . . . Yet, unofficially a certain standard is set that speaks much louder to violators than the welcome sign out front. This standard may be in décor, dress, language or any other area within that church's culture. If you are visiting from outside the particular group (whether the difference is ethnic, social or financial), then you usually understand that you are welcome only if you can conform to the 'comfort zone' of those who govern the system."[27] Outsiders are welcome as long as they mind the "local customs."

Drawing from the horrors of ethnic cleansing and its implications, Volf offers a stronger critique of assimilation. He states, "The more benign side of exclusion by elimination, is exclusion by assimilation. You can survive, even thrive, among us, if you become like us; you can keep your life, if you give up your identity."[28]

Assimilating the minority-population race(s) into the dominant racial culture of the local church community "devalues" what the minority culture brings to the Table and misses an opportunity to grow in Christ. "Because of our lack of exposure to people from other ethnic groups and cultures, we can easily begin to view our own cultures or ethnicity as superior."[29]

Recognizing assimilation can have a detrimental effect on the church, the Evangelical Lutheran Church in America (ELCA) denomination

---

27. Woodley, *Living*, 101.
28. Volf, *Exclusion*, 75.
29. Woodley, *Living*, 102.

declared the following in a social statement concerning race, ethnicity, and culture:

> This church has not moved much beyond an "assimilation" approach to culture, where the assimilated are those who adopt the values and behavior of the dominant culture. This keeps us from benefitting from the plurality of cultures already present in our church, and from appreciating the plurality of cultures in society.
>
> This church clearly shares the brokenness of a society that has responded to cultural diversity through fear and efforts at assimilation. Our society has melded many European ethnic groups into mainstream America, but it has included people of other cultural identities only insofar as they have taken on the values and behavior of the dominant culture.[30]

This is not to say that all assimilation is bad. In some cases, it is necessary. When non-Christians are invited to join the culture (and Body) of Christ, they are expected to give up contrarian beliefs. This type of assimilation demands the exclusion and death of beliefs and attitudes that run counter to a relationship with Christ.[31]

Another example of healthy assimilation is when a multiracial congregation joins with a single race congregation. As in the case of Fellowship of Faith and The Journey, the single race congregation was asked to assimilate into a culture that expands what they had previously been doing.

If assimilation can lead to minimizing or devaluing what others offer through the perspective of their race, ethnicity and culture, what is a healthy alternative to assimilation? DeYoung, Emerson, Yancey, and Chai, describe three categories of multiracial congregations—assimilated, pluralist, and integrated. The assimilation model is characterized by one dominant racial group. "Congregation members who do not belong to that dominant racial group simply "assimilate" into the existing culture. In other words, the way a congregation functions is not significantly changed by the presence of members from different racial groups."[32] The pluralist congregation model gathers different races together as one church and in the same worship service but "members do not move beyond coexistence to real integration of

---

30. Evangelical Lutheran Church in America, "Freed in Christ," lines 78–84.

31. Of course, problems occur when we, as Christians, try to determine what are "essential" beliefs for Christ-followers and contrarian to a relationship with Jesus.

32. DeYoung et al., *United*, 165.

social networks."[33] This form of church incorporates aspects of the different racial cultures into church life and each group participates in shaping the environment and community of the congregation. Yet, "there is little informal social interaction across races . . ."[34]

The integrated congregation "has developed a hybrid of the distinct cultures that have joined together in one church"[35] and there is significant social interaction between races. As the authors describe it, "The relationships among members of different races in the congregation are strictly egalitarian. There is no sense of 'us' and 'them' according to race, but it is more 'us' as a congregation and 'them' outside our congregation."[36] This integrated multiracial congregation model is also described as "accommodation" by DeYmaz and "inclusion" by Garces-Foley.

Accommodation and inclusion are good, but could still allow for separation. These terms imply or assume acceptance but what if this acceptance is reluctant? Acceptance allows for participation, but this author would argue that much more is necessary. A term that seems more apt, and could be supported biblically is "appreciation." It describes a fuller picture of what racial integration can look like in the church. "Appreciation" is intended to imply a sense of mutuality in the relationship or an equal spiritual partnership, "strict egalitarianism", as has been previously described. Moreover, appreciation ascribes value.

As noted previously, because spiritual gifts and salvation experiences are influenced by an individual's background, upbringing and life circumstances, then it seems that the Body of Christ needs other's perspectives on Christ.[37] Because we need to hear about how others have encountered Christ, we can "appreciate" what they offer because it gives a fuller expression for such things as our worship experience and knowledge of God.

Korie Edwards makes a case for a broader understanding of integration. She concludes her book with this exhortation:

> Racial integration is an important component of a racially egalitarian society, but it is not the only one. As churches seek to become interracial, they must not be satisfied with simply having people of different racial groups worship together. They must not even be

33. Ibid., 167.
34. Ibid., 168.
35. Ibid.
36. Ibid.

37. A perspective that can only be known and experienced by those who possess the Holy Spirit.

satisfied with people fellowshipping from time to time outside of church activities. If churches want to realize Dr. King's dream, they must first embrace a dream of racial justice and equality. Interracial churches must be places that all racial groups can call their own, where all racial groups have the power to influence the minor and major decisions of the church, where the culture and experiences of all racial groups are not just tolerated, but appreciated. This demands a radical approach and is certainly a high calling. Whites and racial minorities will have to resist white normativity and structural dominance and fully embrace the cultures, ideas, and perspectives of all racial groups.[38]

Appreciation suggests that what each racial culture offers is valued and worth fighting for. How someone else has encountered and experienced God through the lens of their racial culture benefits me by broadening and deepening my understanding of him. Through the Community of Christ, our relationship to the Eternal Community of Father, Son, and Spirit grows when a brother/sister in Christ reveals to us a previously unknown facet of God.

Unity Must be Intentionally Pursued

Prior to the congregations coming together, OPF took several steps to help create a new identity as one church. Activities included:

- Pulpit exchange—the elders from each church had the opportunity to worship and preach with the other congregation
- Joint worship events—the churches came together to worship and share meals. We had a Seder meal and Christmas program/service together. In a light-hearted comment about change and intercultural relationships, an OPF congregant commented, "I know a few eyebrows were raised when Spam® showed up at potlucks!"
- Fellowship opportunities—there were planned events for having fun together. On a couple of occasions, the women from both congregations met to develop a relationship. Once, they "exchanged recipes" by teaching one another how to make sushi and an American dessert.
- Prayer and ministry—An elder from the other church and the author were involved with starting a monthly prayer ministry that included

38. Edwards, *Elusive*, 140.

two other pastors, one of whom is African-American. The four of us worked to develop a friendship that was intercultural and had a vision for expanding into our local community.

In addition, the elders began relationships with the congregants of the partner churches, taking on the shepherding roles we anticipated once the congregations combined.

Pastor YQ commented that Trinity reinforced the unity of its community by gathering its people around food and ritual. Shortly after the congregations combined, the Korean congregants fixed a Korean meal for the Anglo congregants. The following Easter, the church choir, made up of both Anglos and Koreans, sang a Korean hymn together. The Anglos learned the song phonetically. The guest preacher, himself Korean, said that when he closed his eyes, it sounded like the choir was all Korean.

It's been noted that "all religious expression is embedded in particular cultural forms, so individuals experience God through culturally specified media."[39] Our life experiences inform our worship practice. Recognizing this tendency can head off conflict flashpoints. Christerson, Edwards, and Emerson sum up this religious ethnocentrism saying, "Interracial religious organizations have higher levels of conflict than interracial nonreligious organizations because cultural differences tend to be given absolute and transcendent meanings, making compromise more difficult."[40] Making sacrifices to accommodate others and demonstrating respect for personal preferences can communicate love.

GO, an African-American woman at Philadelphian Community, commented that she was planning to leave because she expected the merge to be political and go poorly, so she had been visiting other churches. One Sunday she came back to visit and said, "I saw something different" about how the Asian congregants were interacting and loving on the older Anglo members. It made a strong impression on her and she stayed.

Instill Fundamental Characteristics of Healthy Multiracial Churches

It takes time and effort to create an environment where people are able to talk about and work through their differences. Priest and Priest report that

---

39. Christerson et al., *Against*, 174.
40. Ibid., 175.

when the vote to merge was taken by the Fellowship and Community congregations, the truth of the problem was revealed. "Believing the merger effort had gone well, Community members were shocked when a deeply divided Fellowship voted two to one against the merger."[41] How could this and similar future situations be avoided? Learning from what works is a good start.

There are essential traits found in multiracial congregations that are needed to create and/or maintain a multiracial community. In chapter 3, Figure 3.1 compiled principles that others deem important to the success of a multiracial church. Figure 6.1 rearranges most of these principles to compare them, showing their correspondence and highlighting the leading components.[42]

Figure 6.1—Principles for a Multiracial Church by Corresponding Attributes

One Body, One Spirit	*People of the Dream*	*Bldg a Healthy MEC*
Diverse leadership	Leaders committed to racial equity	Empower diverse leadership
An overarching goal	Common purpose exceeds racial equity	Embrace dependence
Intentionality	Structures ensure racial equity	Take intentional steps
Personal skills	Institutional commitment to racial equity	Develop cross-cultural relationships
Inclusive worship		Promote a spirit of inclusion
Adaptability	Be a DJ	
	Recognize people are at different places	Pursue cross-cultural competence

---

41. Priest and Priest, "Divergent Worship," 285.

42. The correspondence is not perfect and it could be argued that some principles correspond better with others. This figure is intended to pull common concepts together and show alignment amongst ministry leaders and practitioners. Not every principle is represented because there did not seem to be an appropriate corresponding match.

Key Challenges of Forming Multiracial Congregations through Mergers

In summary, these principles are:

- Diverse leadership
- Christocentric vision
- Deliberate appreciation and value for other perspectives
- Intercultural relationships—relationships, inside and outside of the church, that cross race and culture are foundational.
- Integrative ritual—a worship environment that integrates the different facets of race, ethnicity and culture.
- Leaders sensitive to community dynamics—church leadership needs to be responsive to how relationships and ministry are going within the church. They are attuned to creating an environment of value and respect for what the different groups are bringing to the integrated community.
- Safe learning environment for intercultural relationships—people are at different places on a continuum of a commitment to being multiracial, and it takes time for them to move from one end to the other.[43] To help people grow, they need a setting of grace to make mistakes, learn and understand.

Priest and Priest align with these principles. In their experience of single-race congregations attempting to come together to create a multiracial church, they offer some helpful insights for churches wanting to change their current situation. They ask, "What are some of these lessons for those who wish to constructively engage racial realities?" An abbreviated version of their response[44] follows:

- Culture matters. Shared culture enables effective communication and underpins alignments and solidarities. A lack of shared culture naturally leads to misunderstanding and ethnocentric judgments.
- Good intentions, pure hearts and spiritual disciplines are not enough: "one must acquire adequate social, historical, and cultural understandings as important preconditions underpinning any church-based initiative to bring African Americans and Euro-Americans together."

---

43. Emerson & Woo, *People*, 169.
44. Priest and Priest, "Divergent Worship," 288–89.

- Cultural flexibility, a willingness to learn and participate in other practices, and willingness to signal strong appreciation and affirmation of others and their practices are critical to racial reconciliation.
- Worship practices matter. How people express themselves in worship should be understood to have cultural constraints, and these limitations mean there are alternative, equally valid expressions of worship held by others.
- Leadership matters. Leaders need to be part of a dialogue that crosses racial boundaries and represent the interests of all the racial/ethnic backgrounds.
- Research and writing matter. Churches that are undertaking these challenges of bringing congregations together need to share their experiences with others.

Priest and Priest's insights are consistent with Yancey, Emerson and Woo, and DeYmaz, and lend further understanding to working toward success when joining congregations together. The observations and assertions of these four reference works validate one another by their agreement.

The Leadership Challenge of Multiracial Churches

Van Engen, reflecting on the goal of bringing different races, ethnicities and cultures together, writes:

> In today's multi-ethnic North America, we need to find ways of planting "multi-ethnic" churches where cultural and ethnic differences are affirmed, appreciated, and celebrated. Yet at the same time we are beginning to understand that ethnicity (particularity) as such must not be the basis of unity for these congregations. They are brought together and held together as disciples of Jesus Christ, as the Church. Their basis for unity needs to relate to the *universality* of the Gospel—but that universality must complement rather than eclipse the marvelous richness of ethnic diversity which can be fostered in multi-ethnic congregations.[45]

An ethnically, racially diverse congregation must be the product of what God puts together to reflect who he is and what he has done. Pursuing a multiracial ministry needs to start with God's leading.

45. Van Engen, "Church for Everyone?," 36–37.

Expectations for Leadership

Pastoral roles may change in a church merge. Ministry leaders familiar with merging church congregations advocate the resignation of all pastoral staff. The general opinion is that a belief that a "clean slate" will give the new congregation the best chance at a strong start. In a newly created multiracial congregation, this would be unwise because the pastoral staff will probably be the primary leaders facilitating interpersonal conflict, and the cultural and relational adjustments of the congregants.

In five church pairings, one congregation either had no pastor (Philadelphian, Faith, and OPF) or a pastor planned to retire (The Journey, Trinity). The one church that had both pastors intact, New Creation, experienced a substantial change in leadership—the associate pastor left soon afterwards because of a conflict with the senior pastor.

At OPF, the leadership question was settled by changing the author's role from being a solo pastor to a staff elder. Of the elders, the author was the only one with a paid, full-time position with the church. The primary leadership was comprised of a team of elders, equals in leadership. The preaching is done by a team comprised of elders and members of the congregation. In August 2008, based on our ministry philosophy and goals, the author resigned his staff position and the leadership responsibilities have been distributed amongst the elders (the author remained an elder).

Power shared between the congregations

As noted previously, Laribee recommends that the pastors leave because they may perpetuate the problems that led to creating the merge. This advice fails to consider viable reasons for keeping one or all the pastors around. The pastor(s) may not represent the problems, but be progenitors of the solution. In some cases, churches join together because one congregation is without a minister, and the merge allows for this congregation to gain a shepherd. The strengths of the pastor(s) may be what the new church wants and needs so cutting this out from the ministry may cause more problems than it fixes.

Simmons[46] and Foland[47] share similar concerns because of potential power struggles or inertia that suppresses change. In Simmons' ministry

---

46. Personal interview.
47. Foland, *Beginning*, 71.

experience, both he and the other pastor stayed with the ministry, but over time the differences they had over the church's philosophy of ministry polarized the leadership. Several years after the church merge, Simmons left in order to keep the church unified.

How will the newly formed church accommodate two or more pastors? When churches have a pastoral staff that does not plan to retire or move on, the new church will have to resolve roles. At minimum, the leaders need to be of like mind concerning their respective of understandings of how ministry is done. They need to be realistic about the changes that might need to take place in order for the ministry to grow.

At a broader level, what roles will the leadership of the former congregations have in the new church? Congregants from the respective parent churches will expect to have representation in the new leadership.

It is not simply about giving people equal voting shares or having the same number of elders on the board. What also needs transformation is the public perception of power and control. It is important to have and convey respect to the minority populace of the congregation. Pastor OY describes this process as they helped the Anglo minority make the transition at The Journey: "Part of the transition plan that we drafted also required that I, as the former lead pastor of the IB Church, and some of our other leaders, would be more visible for the first six months. In the preaching and teaching ministries, so I was preaching at least twice a month. At the early service, and it sometimes spilled over to the other service. Some of our musicians were blended in with the worship team." Value and respect will help the racial minority in the new congregation understand they are an integral part of the new ministry.

Leadership needs to be intentionally diversified

The importance of intentional, racially diverse leadership cannot be overstated. The leadership of single-race congregations must change when becoming a multiracial community. It needs to reflect not just the constituency of the church community to be formed, but proactive leadership will try to create a leadership team that reflects what the church strives to become. This is not an affirmative action plan for churches.

DeYmaz writes, "[t]here is no place in the New Testament where quotas are prescribed for leadership within the local church. And attempts to otherwise set them can only be seen as human and therefore flawed, albeit noble, efforts to engineer what we might believe is the greater good. . . . However, we should not expect to integrate our leadership teams through random prayer or wishful thinking. Diverse individuals of godly character, theological agreement, and shared vision do not just arrive on waves of whim. Rather, they must be intentionally sought."[48] DeYmaz does not advocate bringing unqualified people into leadership roles for the sake of diversity. A person may be unqualified but they can, and should, receive training and mentoring that equips them for a leadership role.

No one would suggest that the qualifications of leadership roles need to be compromised in order to accomplish diversity. But creating diversity may challenge perceptions concerning what qualifies one for leadership. For instance, if a parent church has, as a practice only lets seminary-educated men preach from the pulpit, then what will happen if they join with a congregation that has a different set of values concerning women or graduate education?

Multiracial ministry will shake up the structure and operation of leadership. Fong points out, "It is difficult for ethnics to believe that a church is eager to display the reconciliation of Christ in a multi-cultural community when all of the church leadership are of the majority or controlling culture. Transition time for maturing of leaders is one matter, but, it cannot be a permanent excuse. Racial minorities are too familiar with such excuses."[49] He continues "'power' [can be] a primary blockade to true racial reconciliation in the church."

Edwards offers significant insights about the nature of multiracial churches, especially the racial dynamic involving African-American and Anglo congregants. On the diversity of leadership, she comments, "When it comes to leadership structure in interracial churches, race matters both symbolically and culturally. That is, the actual race of key leaders in interracial church is important . . ."[50]

48. DeYmaz, *Building*, 74.

49. Fong, *Racial Equality*, 161.

50. Edwards, *Elusive*, 81. In context, she makes key observations about power in an interracial church. Because Anglos are the dominant culture, racial minorities may need 'white cultural capital' to function effectively within a particular cultural setting.

1 + 1 = 1

Leadership Requires Vision, Not Pragmatism

In an unintentionally humorous exchange, a newspaper reported the formation of a multiracial church in Atlanta, GA. Responding to a question about why their two churches were coming together to form a multiracial ministry, this is what the two pastors had to say:

> "Why not?" said the Rev. C.J. Chun [pastor of Korean and Chinese congregation]. "We believe in the same God. There's no reason why we shouldn't worship together. It's just a matter of racial differences and color differences." The Rev. Chris Robins [pastor of the Anglo congregation] agreed. "If we truly embrace the idea that we are all of one people and members of one collective Christian body, then our houses of worship should demonstrate it," he said.[51]

"Why not" is hardly a compelling reason and it lacks staying power, especially when conflicts start popping up. Whether these pastors were misquoted or this is the depth of their understanding about multiracial ministry, bringing congregations together must be more than a good idea or a pragmatic action. "The questions about how the merged congregations will function can actually thwart a possible merger if there is no clear and inspiring vision and compelling sense of mission. Vision and mission come first."[52]

A key aspect that contributed to OPF forming was having a vision big enough to motivate people to follow. The perception that there would be too much change (philosophy of ministry, leadership, meeting time, and location) led to fears that overwhelmed the process. The vision the elders had touted was muddled by a competing desire to keep people happy and reassure them that the change was not going to be that bad. The leadership wanted everyone to embrace the merge and stay together. However, change was going to be disruptive and a vision that would justify the discomfort was needed. The imagery of Rev 7:9 was persuasive and brought clarity to the effort. Many from both congregations were excited by the picture of what Heaven will be like.

Leadership's commitment to the vision also demands resolve. At some point in time, the congregations will go from "dating" to "committing to a relationship." The decision to make a commitment to join congregations together is critical.

51. Quinn, "Midtown," lines 6–11.
52. Foland, *Beginning*, 66–67.

Key Challenges of Forming Multiracial Congregations through Mergers

When the decision to integrate congregations has been made, OPF's experience suggests that the leadership should commit themselves to their new vision and accept the consequences (i.e., people leave). If the vision and mission of the new church is according to God's plan and call, then pursuing anything else is foolish. The temptation to keep everyone together and not harm longstanding relationships is very real.

Vision inspires hope

Part of "selling" the vision involves describing it in terms that people can understand, and with imagery that describes a persuasive end result. In his book about transitioning organizations, Bridges shares the story of a business that was closing a manufacturing plant and needed to reframe the perception that things were coming to a dismal end for the plant and its people.

> This talk about metaphors—about a "sinking ship" versus a "last voyage"—may seem like mere word-play. But the words are labels on two completely different ways of looking at a difficult situation. The new metaphor of a last voyage didn't invalidate the difficulty— that was a given. But it gave a purpose to the situation, while the old metaphor left people felling hopeless. The new metaphor carried the message "Make the most of this situation," while the old metaphor told people, "Get out of here as fast as you can."[53]

A biblical metaphor can link the process of merging to a theological foundation. Exhorting God's people to change should be framed by concepts connected to Scripture.

McClendon found that a good metaphor helped congregations understand the merge better.[54] Most frequently, marriage was used to describe the relationship[55], but McClendon adds birth, as well as death and resurrection for consideration. Laribee prefers a garden[56] over marriage paralleling McClendon's death and resurrection analogy. Yanagihara likens the merge to "a new creation."

---

53. Bridges, *Transitions*, 45.
54. McClendon, "Minefield," 159.
55. As described by Alan W. Black, Gregg, and McClendon.
56. Laribee, "Factors," 108.

The marriage analogy has its limits, especially because of the number of people involved.[57] In this ministry situation, two become one but they are bringing their respective families together. Local members of the family of Christ joining together end up creating a new household that resembles a blended family.

In two of the churches surveyed (Philadelphian Community and Fellowship of Faith), a larger, healthier church took over the smaller ministry. While the smaller congregations were declining in number and aging, they owned a building and had material assets that would help the resulting congregation. They generously gave away what they had to give the new ministry a home, and took on the burden of enduring the greatest amount of change. These particular ministries modeled sacrifice, which, as a metaphor, is an intimidating, costly image. In many respects, "sacrifice" is apt if both congregations involved live up to biblical imagery.

OPF described the church merge as a rebirth. We wanted to convey that both parent congregations would cease and begin anew as a new ministry. Calling the coming together a "'rebirth' was an important driver for us" because it reframed how the congregants should view what was happening. The importance of capturing and conveying an image that described what we were attempting was critical. Recalling what he was thinking at the time of our rebirth, Pastor PN put it this way, "For me, I wasn't interested in a merge and I'm not interested in a merge. I would choose the word rebirth because it puts before me a vision of what I can become, . . . what we can become. Not what we are because what we are hasn't worked. What we are has come to a dead end. What we are, if we don't change, will be extinct."

Members of each church were invited to be a part of creating what the new church would become. We wanted to avoid a situation where the planning teams "negotiated" what would be retained or discarded. There were elements of compromise on issues of preference, but the overarching notion was that we were, in effect, starting from scratch. The idea would be akin to what Jesus describes of a seed needing to die in order to produce much fruit.[58] The churches contributing to the formation of OPF had to die in order to move forward with a new ministry.

---

57. In our case, jokes about polygamy made this metaphor much less appealing.
58. John 12:24.

Key Challenges of Forming Multiracial Congregations through Mergers

Conflict Is an Opportunity to Cultivate Unity

Conflict is going to happen, especially when bringing different racial cultures together. How people view Christ, particularly through the lens of one's upbringing can lead to strong opinions and preferences. Brad Christerson observes, "What makes these conflicts difficult is that in a faith environment people tend to talk about cultural differences in absolute terms, making compromise difficult. For example, something as minor as how rigidly you time the church service can lead to major conflict.... In a faith environment, cultural differences quickly become conflicts over what is the 'godly' or 'biblical' way of doing things."[59]

About seven months into the dialogue and planning for coming together, the plan to create OPF came to an abrupt halt.[60] A few members of GCC Church were concerned that aspects of GCC's ministry would change by joining with FBC (i.e., loss of relational intimacy, a move toward spiritual superficiality). Believing that this was a widespread concern, the leadership of GCC pulled away from the joint venture. Within a month of the expressed worries, the plan to join churches was dead. In frustration, one of the elders at FBC resigned his position and announced his family would leave.

Through the summer, the remaining elders worked through what had happened. Reviewing a time-line of events and conversations, we realized that the decision to step away from bringing our churches together was based more on how we thought people would respond rather than pursuing what God wanted. Recognizing our error, we went back to our congregations, and confessed our mistake and lack of faith. We asked for their forgiveness and asked our people to pursue the original vision we set—to join the two churches. The time and energy spent discovering and owning the elders' weaknesses and faults, and mending relationships served to draw us (the elders and the churches) closer together.

Racial reconciliation is an important conflict to deal with directly. The approach should certainly be tactful and mutually edifying. The issue of race relations should be part of the conversation at the church.[61] A weakness of ethnic transcendence is that subordinating or "ignoring" racial con-

---

59. Kinoshita, "Heaven," 9.

60. The decision to call off the rebirth began in April 2005 and was not resolved until September 2005 when the plan was revived with everyone rallying around a bigger vision.

61. Emerson and Woo, *People*, 169.

flict is an unhealthy way to handle conflict. The problem does not go away; it just receives less priority. By definition, reconciliation entails dealing with a conflict and restoring the relationship because each one has "owned" their part in the breakdown of the relationship.[62]

Conflict can be catalytic for improving relationship because it offers an avenue for moving beyond superficial interaction. People are less inclined to fight over small things or issues they are indifferent about. On the other hand, because people will take a stand on things important to them, resolving closer to the heart issues in a healthy fashion can bring about a deeper understanding and appreciation for what another person values.

Ken Sande describes peoples' understanding of conflict this way: "To some, conflict is a hazard that threatens to sweep them off their feet and leave them bruised and hurting. To others, it is an obstacle that they should conquer quickly and firmly. But a few people have learned that conflict is an opportunity to solve common problems in a way that honors God and offers benefits to those involved."[63] If conflict is viewed as part of the process of relationship building, as opposed to attack-and-counterattack or negotiation, it can serve to reinforce relational bridges.

The Integration Challenge when Joining Churches Together

The Church Planter's Toolkit proposes ten methods for starting churches—pioneering, branching, colonizing, seeding, adopting, partnering, revitalizing, transplanting, propagating and catalyzing. Surprisingly, merging is not a consideration. This omission may be indicative of how it is viewed as a means of growing God's kingdom.

This strategy for starting new churches is not limited to "last chance" scenarios. The view that church mergers are the action of last resort is a function of tradition and status quo rather than thoughtful deliberation.

In contrast, this book asserts that joining churches together is a solid, viable alternative to planting a church. Given the scope of the work, it is very much like planting a church. The starting conditions are different, but there are many common attributes. At the least, merging churches deserves consideration as another method for starting churches.

---

62. Matt 6:21–26 and 18:15–22 both describe Jesus' perspective on resolving conflict issues.

63. Sande, *Peacemaker*, 17.

Key Challenges of Forming Multiracial Congregations through Mergers

Joining churches together can be a means for transforming and revitalizing ministries, as in the case of a number of denominations.[64] Using the vernacular of the present day's concern for the environment, it might even be viewed as "recycling" churches—something old is made new again. From a biblical perspective, a church merger offers a ministry solution that is visionary and redemptive.

Based on the type of work that has been done on church mergers, denomination-focused research and dissertations make up a significant portion of these studies. It is possible that denominations consider merging options because they have invested in a ministry (property), visibility to congregations looking for help, developed a level of expertise to share throughout the denomination, and significant resources at their disposal (interim and merger-experienced pastoral staff).

Of the numerous works on church growth reviewed, Jones is the only one who gives substantive thought to church mergers. It is possible that the reason church mergers receive scant attention is because there have been few successes. With a strong correlation between change and conflict, church mergers, considered the epitome of radical change, are expected to have much conflict. Laribee writes, "a merger of two or more organizations most likely will be the largest collection of simultaneous changes that a congregation may ever experience. Often, only the death of the organization would be more traumatic than merger, and then perhaps only slightly more traumatic."[65] The anticipation of conflict may lead to foregone conclusions of failure.

Stating the obvious, it seems odd that churches struggle with conflict when they have the ultimate Model of conflict resolution in Jesus.

Merging as a Response to External Forces

Emerson notes that ministries may change from monoracial to multiracial because pressures outside of the church prompt the need for change. He explains, "two main factors appear to underlie the manner in which multiracial congregations develop: (1) the primary impetus for becoming a multiracial congregation . . . and (2) the source of the minority population (environment)."[66]

64. As per Gregg, McClendon and Yanagihara.
65. Laribee, "Factors," 79–80.
66. Emerson and Woo, *People*, 53.

1 + 1 = 1

The goal prompting change may be the result of the church's mission (its reason for existence), resource calculation (the resources that will build or sustain the ministry) or external authority structure (denominational leadership dictates change).[67] Furthermore, the diversification of the congregation may be fueled by proximity ("an available population of racially different persons from which to draw new members...."[68]), its purpose and culture, or preexisting churches ("The membership diversity comes from the joining together of preexisting congregations, not by an increase in new membership."[69]).

Figure 6.2[70] describes how change may occur, and illustrates the type of multiracial congregations that form from the reasons for change and the source of diversification.

Figure 6.2—Impetus for Change, Diversification Source, and Multiracial Congregational Types

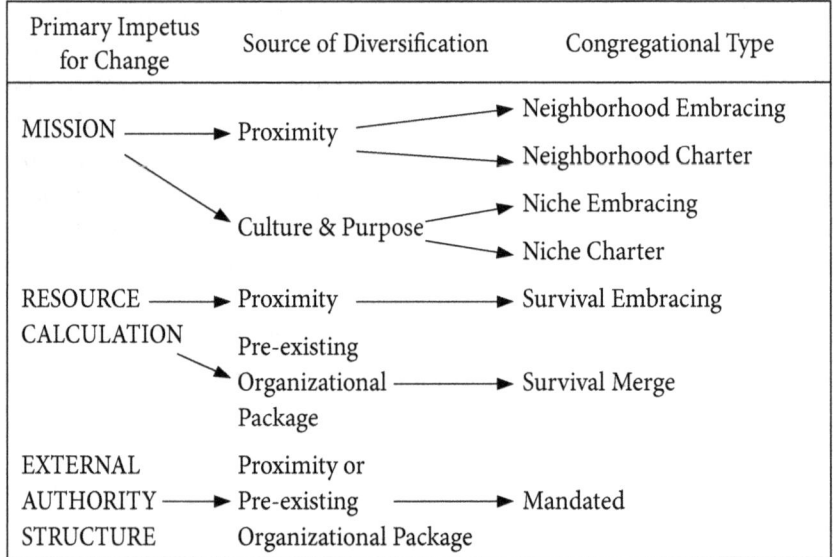

---

67. Ibid., 53–54.
68. Ibid., 54.
69. Ibid., 55.
70. *Note.* Adapted from Figure 3.1 from *People of the Dream* by Emerson and Woo, 2006, p. 56. Copyright 2006 by Michael O. Emerson and Rodney M. Woo. Reprinted with permission from Princeton University Press.

Key Challenges of Forming Multiracial Congregations through Mergers

Emerson notes that multiple causes may contribute to forming a multiracial congregation, but there is usually a primary reason that factors more heavily than the others.

The congregational type refers to how the church acquires its congregation. If it is "embracing" it forms because of the change going on in the community around it, and it changes to accept the people who are in the area. If it is a "charter", its ministry has been established from its inception. A "merge" is the combining of congregations. A "mandated" congregation "originates not from internal decisions, but from decisions made by an authority structure outside the congregation."[71]

There is nothing inherently wrong with churches forming because they want to keep going; after all, a church community is founded on relationship. However, in creating an updated vision for the church, the ministry should be pursuing a God-given vision versus being with people we like or meeting a market demand. The vision for change may have a divine or pragmatic source.

McLendon comes to a similar conclusion, describing it this way:

> Church merger should not be seen as a means to the end of institutional survival. The impetus for this form of radical change must be love for others, not desire for self-preservation. . . . Spiritual renewal must be one of the primary reasons for merger if it is to have hope of success. The pastoral leader must help move the emphasis of members to reasons higher than survival or financial benefits. Churches should merge because Christian disciples have God-assigned tasks to do and they may be better able to do them together.[72]

Based on his experience with approximately seventy efforts to merge congregations, Foland believes that there are three primary motivations that will only forestall closure—survival, pastors who seem to work well together and hoping to create a more efficient ministry. Because these reasons lack a persuasive vision there is little to keep the new church from failing. He argues, "Mergers should be approached not primarily as a solution to problems, but on the basis of the gifts and assets each congregation brings to the table. Mergers will work best when the potential partners carefully assess the assets they can bring to a new beginning. Merger might

---

71. Emerson and Woo, *People*, 60.
72. McClendon, "Minefield," 58.

be motivated by desperate situations, but lasting mergers of congregations are the result of a good blend of gifts each partner has to offer for new mission."[73]

In the case of Trinity Church, the ministry they fell apart because the ministry could not overcome the trial of keeping the congregation together by working through conflict and resolving it in a healthy fashion. The work to come together was seen as a way to rescue both parent congregations. Because the perceived end goal was attained, sustaining the ministry was harder than they expected.

The leadership had loftier desires, as noted in a local paper interview of the founding pastors (Kim is the Korean pastor):

> Kim sees the goal of the new church clearly.
>
> "The ultimate goal for this ministry is to become a multicultural ministry," Kim said. In the meantime, he said the goal is to become bicultural. But including other ethnicities will be in the church's future.
>
> Kim said there have been "some successes, some failures" when it comes to combining the two cultures in worship.
>
> "This is not a problem," he said, "it's an opportunity. The most important thing is communication between the two leaders of the church first and the two congregations. It's a pioneering ministry."
>
> Kim admitted that for some of the older generation of Koreans in his congregation, there "has been some confusion, some negative feelings."
>
> "But in knowing first generation immigrant Korean people," Kim continued, "I could understand this, because their social activities are limited to the Korean community. They are in a very unfamiliar situation. For second-generation Korean children, they are very happy. They are the future of our church. I think we have to focus on them.[74]

Given how the venture ended, the interview reveals some of what the pastor did not see. While Trinity Church had a vision to reach their local community as an example of reconciliation, there were underlying motives that went unfilled—the Korean congregation wanted a building of their own. Internal conflict that the Korean pastor hoped would be replaced by a "higher" goal was not.

---

73. Foland, *Beginning*, 66.
74. Riegel, "New Life-Eastminster," page 2.

The Alternatives to Church Mergers Are More Attractive

To be honest, church mergers are difficult work and the alternatives, church planting in its various forms, sound more appealing. Wagner offers six reasons for new churches, he notes that they are: key and vital for outreach, have better spiritual health than older churches, increase the opportunities to reach the unchurched, are needed because many places are underchurched, sustain denominations by replacing dying churches, and minister to other believers.[75] Aubrey Malphurs has a similar opinion and observes that the advantages a new church has over an established one is faster growth, better evangelism, greater leadership credibility, and more flexibility from the congregation.

On the face of it, a "new" church looks preferable because it is easier to assemble a team of like-minded individuals to create the desired church environment—aligning ministry components such as polity, doctrine, philosophy of ministry, corporate worship, Bible studies, home groups, and youth and children programs. The negatives against church mergers make church plants even more attractive. Stuart Murray makes church merges akin to pouring money down a hole. He believes:

> The very features that might be regarded as advantages are sadly often the reasons why no amount of investment of energy and personnel will achieve the desired goals. Many struggling churches are saddled with: inadequate or inappropriate buildings, indebtedness, poor community relations, debilitating traditions, intransigent leaders and low morale. The loyalty and perseverance of members of these congregations may be undeniable, but attempts to prolong the life of such churches may be based more on sentimentality and a maintenance orientation than on seeking first the kingdom of God and reaching out effectively in mission to the surrounding community.[76]

In addition, when bringing congregations together the leadership needs to consider potential organizational and personal flashpoints (among a range of other issues), encourage and assist people with change, and work with reluctant congregants.

---

75. Wagner, *Harvest*.
76. Murray, *Foundations*, 11.

Schaller is pessimistic about church merges as well. In his opinion, based on hundreds of cases, merges do not do very well.[77] His dismal assessment is not meant to discourage, but to caution: "These comments do not mean that every merger is doomed to produce disappointments. The history of both congregational and denominational mergers since 1950, however, suggests that an excessively simplistic approach is likely to demonstrate that two plus two does not automatically equal four."[78] Given his experience, the warning is justified. Churches attempting this venture should go in with eyes wide open, expecting the road to be rough.

To use a different analogy, a new car is much more attractive than an old, used car. It has less miles on it, a warranty, and the latest features (e.g., safety, comfort, mileage, and styling). It also has a different price tag. The costs and merits of the "old car" follow in the next chapter, "Opportunities of this Ministry Approach."

Engender Factors for Success

There are common threads in the observations made concerning what makes a merge "successful." The literature and surveys indicate that there are particular fundamentals that are indispensable.

Not surprisingly, the elements that make a church merge successful are also necessary for success in multiracial ministry. Distilling these elements, the core essentials that give a multiracial church merge a strong foundation are:

Vision—clear, God-given, and christocentric

Leadership—courageous, has a conviction about and is committed to racial diversity and integration, and merging

Communication—clear, consistent, and frequent

Change and conflict management—anticipates and manages transition and conflict

Taking the principles that are important to a multiracial church (from Figure 6. 1) and linking them to the elements that are vital to a church merge produces a framework that might look like Figure 6.3.

77. Schaller, *Reflections*, 140.
78. Ibid., 141.

Key Challenges of Forming Multiracial Congregations through Mergers

Figure 6.3—Framework for Multiracial Merge Process

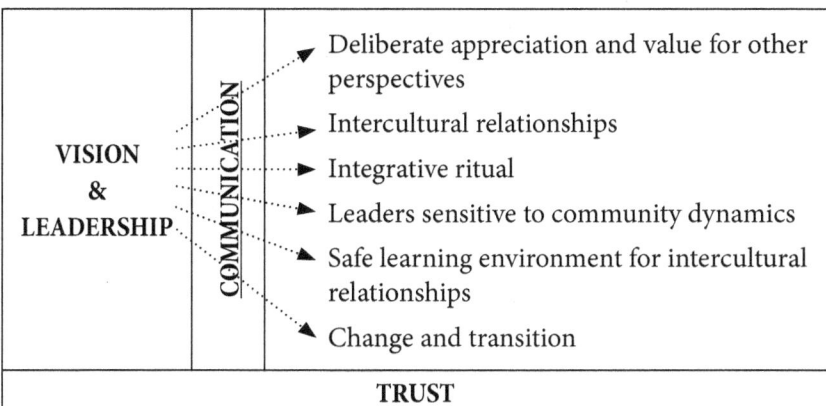

Trust is critical and undergirds the relationships within the church. It allows leadership to guide people through transition, conflict and change. For the congregation to move forward, it needs to be able to trust the ability and heart of leadership—that the leaders are pursuing God's mission for the new ministry, looking out for the people under their care, and providing direction and opportunities for their participation in the work of ministry. The process for bringing congregations together and creating a multiracial community is built upon a foundation of trust.

Leadership develops the vision, mission, and core values for the ministry. These elements driving the ministry, in turn, determine what leadership will look like and dictate what it will and will not do.

Vision and leadership represent and implement what will happen in the ministry. The principles necessary for a multiracial church and a church merge are shaped by the vision and regularly communicated by leadership.[79]

Communication is significant because it conveys information and expresses empathy and care. In a report on congregational merges for

---

79. For further consideration on the progression of this process, Emerson identifies Alan Parker's Ph.D. dissertation as providing a useful description of the stages of development uniracial congregations go through as they evolve into multiracial congregations. Very briefly, the stages are: 1) Status Quo—demographic change occurs but has little impact on the church, 2) Assimilation and Hegemony—diversity increases but newcomers are expected to assimilate, 3) Limited Integration—the leadership begins to diversify and new groups are gaining a voice, 4) Integration and Disintegration—the original group has declined in size and things begin to change as integration occurs, and 5) Stabilization and Reorganization—the congregation has taken on a new identity as a multiracial church (Emerson and Woo, *People*, 171).

synagogues, Harvey Brenner found it was necessary to prepare people for uncertainty and assure them that change is coming.[80] He states, "Congregations must also be made aware that mergers are instruments of change and are specifically designed to not preserve the status quo. The most successful mergers, in fact, do just the opposite, they obliterate the "what is" and replace it with a new (and hopefully better) "what might be." Merger, therefore, is the antithesis of maintaining the status quo and is counterproductive to its preservation and restoration."[81] The sooner people are encouraged to "deal in reality," recognize the situation they are in and what they are aspiring to, the easier the transition will be.

Humility builds trust

The value and power of humility is vital to creating relationships of trust.

In the interview with Pastor OY, the author was struck by how self-effacing he was as he related the story of how The Journey came about. What he shared was matter-of-fact and did nothing to draw extra attention to his role in the process. Yet, from my perspective, it was his leadership that made the whole thing possible. Pastor BZ, the senior pastor at The Journey, recognizes the gift he and his congregation received and he graciously acknowledges what has taken place. The partnership between these two leaders provides a model and testimony to their congregation.

The willingness of the older congregants (at Trinity, Philadelphian and The Journey) to relinquish ownership of their buildings and ministry is, in my opinion, quite remarkable. They have not only given a material gift to a younger generation but the humility they embody is priceless.

Congregants blessed with leadership that demonstrates humility are more likely to trust their leaders because they have shown themselves to be trustworthy in an area (pride) that all wrestle with. Likewise, leaders can bless one another by being willing to relinquish preferences concerning ministry. Strong opinions concerning leadership, polity, worship, evangelism, and ministry, in general, will lead to conflict when leaders do not share these views.

---

80. Brenner, *Merging*, 18.
81. Ibid., 12.

Be Alert to Factors of Failure

Failure is more than the absence of successful components (e.g., a lack of vision, poor communication or unplanned leadership). The research indicates that the obstacles to a merge include incompatible non-negotiables (things that a congregation cannot and will not concede or relinquish), attrition, the "fear of losing congregational identity; loyalty to existing congregation and its history, affection for church building or property, interpersonal conflicts resulting from changes, and fear of change."[82]

Schaller details a number of barriers to a healthy merge.[83] He observes that conflicts that prevent the merge from doing well come about when:

- The new congregation's culture does not change. The church does not organizationally plan for growth, so the numerically larger church still functions as its smaller predecessors did.
- Doctrinal and theological views of the parent congregations differ.
- Substantial ethnic or nationality differences are present.
- Crossing social class lines.
- Philosophies of ministry are disparate.
- Leadership abilities differ and there is a jockeying for power.
- Disagreement over what holds and keeps the congregation together relationally (i.e.—personality of pastor, ministry program, cultural heritage, role in church, spiritual experience).

Schaller's list is understandable, but the differences regarding ethnicity and nationality are worth ignoring for this ministry context—working across racial and social boundaries is an imperative for multiracial churches.

If unresolved problems and issues in the parent congregations are not dealt with, they could very well become recurring issues in the new congregation.[84] When a church fails to address its real problems and is only concerned with survival, "the old patterns and habits of the churches continue and the culture of the merged congregation contains the seeds for destruction. Putting together two congregations that have both been in serious decline and denial about why they have been in decline will not bring

---

82. McClendon, "Minefield," 97.
83. Schaller, *Reflections*, 142–43.
84. Laribee, "Factors," 83.

about the necessary changes to foster growth and generate new energy or vitality."[85] Problems that plagued a church beforehand will continue if they are not settled.

---

85. Foland, *Beginning*, 65.

7

Opportunities of This Ministry Approach

CREATING A MULTIRACIAL MINISTRY by consolidating monoracial churches should be given serious, prayerful consideration. It is a ministry strategy that advances God's kingdom at several levels. The difficulty of this work means success is depends upon God not chance or human ingenuity and ability.

Forming a multiracial church from single race congregations demonstrates conciliation between people as Christians and across race. In a society where race is a touchy issue and a barometer of social mores (e.g., Barack Obama running for President of the United States and winning the election), how the church approaches and handles this subject is laden with opportunity. As Eric Holder, US Attorney General, asserted, "Though this nation has proudly thought of itself as an ethnic melting pot, in things racial we have always been and I believe continue to be, in too many ways, essentially a nation of cowards."[1]

This ministry approach offers a solution to the future demands and needs of a changing population in the United States. The rate of growth of racial minority groups suggests promising prospects for evangelism, service and cross-cultural relationships.

A multiracial merge is a reasonable alternative to planting a church, and can be a healthy way to transform or revitalize a ministry. McClendon reports that over 70 percent of pastors and nearly 75 percent of congregants who participated in a church merger[2] would agree that it is a desirable strategy for starting a new faith community.

---

1. Barrett, "Holder," lines 4–5.
2. McClendon's sample population covered seven churches and he had 273 responses.

Integrating Race and Congregations is Redemptive

Merging churches can advance the kingdom by modeling redemption. Summing up what has already been discussed, this redemption occurs at several levels:

1. The churches undertaking the process have an opportunity to be revitalized through change.
2. Racial reconciliation is lived out and modeled when previously segregated races are integrated.
3. Resources (i.e., finances, people, spiritual gifting, and property) that were previously unavailable become accessible.
4. The resources required to join churches together are less likely to draw resources from other churches, especially in the way of transfer growth.
5. The church community that models reconciliation offers an example of relational restoration.

Revitalizes through Change

Congregations considering joining with another are not necessarily thinking that the status quo will be maintained. They have a vested interest in seeing the new church thrive, and the members of the congregations want an opportunity for rejuvenation. Merging churches offers discouraged congregants new hope. Hadaway's report states, "The mere presence of older adults is not problematic in and of itself. But a congregation where a large proportion of the members are older tends to have a cluster of characteristics that inhibit growth. Not only are no children being born to members, but such congregations tend to lack a clear sense of mission and purpose, vibrant worship or involvement in recruitment/evangelism . . ."[3] A church merge would bring about direction and purpose.

Furthermore, in contrast to the view that age hinders change, age is an asset. The wisdom of age can enhance the depth of how a younger congregation experiences Christ. Given the attitudes of some racial and ethnic populations concerning the elderly, the viability of older Anglo

---

3. Hadaway, *FACTs*, 3.

Opportunities of This Ministry Approach

congregations joining together with younger, racial/ethnic congregations increases because of this cultural dynamic.

For OPF, joining another church was a way to revive both parent congregations that had reached a plateau. We brought our congregations together because we needed to shift what we were doing. The Asian church was formed to minister to non-immigrant Asians assimilated into American culture. We needed and wanted something bigger than this. The opportunity to join with another congregation allowed us to reorient our ministry. For us, instrumental to this change was the promise of and value for older believers who had experienced more than we understood. We wanted a ministry environment that was both multiracial and intergenerational, and the prospect of being able to have this generated enthusiasm for the process.

Churches involved with creating a new church community have an opportunity to be revitalized through the changes brought about by the merge.

Models Racial Reconciliation

As the congregations join together, intercultural dialogue to understand one another will be an integral part of the unification process.

The Journey took a proactive approach to initiating dialogue between races for the community and their church.[4] Annually, they offer a series of meetings on faith and race which are open to the public. The meetings allow participants "to learn more about racism in America, deepen our understanding of what it means to call ourselves a 'multiethnic church.'" The Journey supplements lectures with video clips from *Color of Fear*, books and articles on race issues, and small group discussions led by its members.

As reported by their city's local newspaper, the faith and race class explored reasons for segregation in the church and how the church can respond. The goal of these classes and dialogues is to work toward solutions that impact people personally and their church as an institution.[5]

Working through these issues can attract attention and allow these churches to inspire change in their community. Unity Baptist Church in St. Paul, MN, became an influential model in their city.

---

4. QC, "Faith & Race."
5. Iwasaki, "Faith," line 4.

1 + 1 = 1

> For Unity members and clergy, working toward reconciliation not only means bridging racial divisions inside the church, but being a model and an agitator in the community. It means working with Cub Foods to hire people of color from the city instead of bussing workers in from the suburbs. It means asking the two former churches' denominations, the progressive National Baptist Church which is black, and the American Baptist Church which is white, to work collaboratively in their dealings with Unity. It even means suggesting to news organizations that a white and black reporter work in tandem when doing a profile of the church. Pastor Johnson says the demands of being a member of a church of reconciliation are enormous.

Pastor Dave Johnson adds, "It changes their relationships with their friends, with their families, it means that people on the job are asked to talk about race. Going to a seminar, people ask them to say what their experiences are because they are supposed to be examples of reconciliation. So each person, just coming to that worship experience, is forced to become an ambassador of reconciliation the rest of their lives."[6] The way to become a "city on the hill" is to be a model in the community.

Apart from God's perspective, mixing races does not seem to make sense, especially when people prefer to be with others like themselves. Therefore, the church models how things can be when God is involved. Visser t'Hooft wrote,

> Under certain conditions ethnic Churches may be justified for purely practical reasons, but these must under no circumstances be held to be the true pattern of the Church, for they are abnormal rather than normal, we should moreover guard against the danger of cresting anachronistic Churches, that is Churches which seek to keep a language or culture alive in an artificial manner when the situation really demands the adoption of a more widely used language and the integration of a cultural minority group into a wider cultural context. In any case the linguistic or cultural argument must never be used as a pretext for a purely racial form of segregation. In the racial field the Churches are not to follow the slow pace of society, but to set the example for what human relationships are meant to be. The Churches must therefore resolutely face the implications of their own message and mission, even if this involves a conflict with the mores of their environment.[7]

---

6. Roberts, "Reconciliation," lines 55–63.
7. Visser t'Hooft, *Racial Problem*, 65.

Opportunities of This Ministry Approach

The church can and should show the world the power of Christ's redemption in the relationships between people across racial divides.

Maximizes Resource Distribution

Resources (i.e., finances, people, spiritual gifting, and property) that were previously unavailable become accessible. These resources, given to God's people to build up the Body of Christ, can be redistributed within the new congregation. In this way, more members of the Body are built up. The resources that had been limited to one church are now shared by the larger community.

In the majority of the merges, one of the parent congregations found a home as a result of the congregations coming together. Having a place to meet, a substantial resource, is often important to a ministry. Because the facilities in these merger examples were owned by older congregations, the property was paid off and the cost of leasing space was not exchanged for paying down a mortgage. This freed a significant portion of revenue to be used for other ministry purposes.

Relationally, mixing generations allows younger and older to minister to one another. In the churches studied, "old" and "young" congregations merged understanding that there would be a significant benefit for each of the generations. The younger congregants would benefit from the wisdom and experience of the older. The older congregants would have people to build into and younger blood to take up aspects of the ministry that are not kind to age (e.g., manual labor on the church grounds, working with junior high aged boys or toddlers).

Minimizes Resource Dispersion

The resources going into joining churches together is less likely to draw resources from other churches, especially in the way of transfer growth. Churches that join together to consolidate their resources and revitalize a ministry are distinct from church plants. Start-up churches can sometimes take members away from existing ministries, especially if they do not receive support from a mother church. Pastor YZ described a church plant that took people away from his church and other local churches, and created ill feelings toward the leadership of the church plant.

In his book, *Stealing Sheep*, William Chadwick describes a "dirty little secret" of the church growth movement—it promotes transfer growth. "Yet hidden in the recesses of his work were three principles that would lead to justification of transfer growth. In the years following McGavran's seminal publications, these three principles would be absorbed into the mainstream philosophies of the church growth movement."[8] While not an opponent of church growth, Chadwick is willing to explore its weaknesses. A primary concern is that church plants grow by the unintended and intended consequences of transfer growth.[9]

In addition, church plants that are start-ups can redirect money from existing ministries. The financial support to sustain a church plant may not come from a foundation or denomination, but from friends of those starting the ministry. The money that infuses the start-up is "new" money that is possibly being "redirected" from another ministry, whereas a church merge in all likelihood will fund itself.

Because of how church mergers form, they do not pin their establishment on "new bodies," but instead rely on existing members. Furthermore, rather than moving people, along with their spiritual gifts, passions, and financial support, from one congregation to another, church mergers keep people and their resources in-house. All the church consolidations surveyed in this study provided an opportunity to share people, property and financial assets. This strengthened the new ministry and put resources to profitable use when they might have been squandered or lost if the church merge had not taken place.

Transfer growth is detrimental to the local church and hazardous to the health of the Body of Christ. When church becomes a commodity, some churches will suffer because they may be perceived as offering an inferior product prompting its "customers" to leave. Leith Anderson states that "the greatest factor in denominational decline is the rise of consumerism and consumer advocacy in American culture."[10]

Not only does a consumerist perspective encourage transfer growth, it promotes racial and class homogeneity. Paul Louis Metzger gives notice about its threat to the Body of Christ:

8. Chadwick, *Stealing Sheep*, 83.

9. An example of this can be seen when church plants recruit their core team or core families from people attending other churches. In addition, the church planter neglects to inform or interact with other churches' leadership about the "conversations" the planter is having with their congregants.

10. Anderson, *Dying*, 49.

The consumerist mindset entails giving consumers what they want, when they want it, and at the least cost to consumers themselves. It also creates in consumers the desire to want, and then to want more, even to want things they did not originally want—programming them to buy a given product in the free-market system. Such catering to what consumers want and creating wants in order to win them over to buying a given product is socially acceptable today, even in the church.

The consumerist, free-market spirit disguises itself as an angel of light. However, it cleverly shapes race and class divisions in the evangelical church and beyond, and it makes conquering these depersonalizing and dehumanizing forces increasingly difficult.[11]

Church attendance based on a "what's-in-it-for-me" attitude moves people from church to church as they look for a place that best meets their perceived needs. Church plants may unintentionally contribute to the whims of "church shoppers."

Merging congregations is an alternative that does not minister to perceived needs but offers a recharge to the congregations "rebooting" themselves. The emphasis in merging is about giving congregations/people a "new" chance. People who God can still work on are invited to participate in a renewal of themselves and their church. Transfer growth lets churches die because the "able-bodied" will leave behind the "sick." Churches on "life support" have an opportunity to be redeemed and renewed by church mergers.

Models Relational Reconciliation

Closely related to racial reconciliation, the restoration of relationships in general is important. The nature of multiracial congregations invites conflict. No one has to look for it because it will find you.

Conflict will happen and the process of working through relational difficulties brings about growth for the parties involved and the church. Additionally, it can be a catalyst for redemptive relationships with those outside of the church.

As observed in some of these merge situations, the new and/or parent church may experience a decline in attendance because of how the transition process was managed (e.g., too much change, conflict with

---

11. Metzger, *Consuming Jesus*, 40.

other congregants, or leadership was perceived as unbending, uncaring, or unresponsive). The opportunity to restore relationships with former congregants is possible if they see and/or hear things are handled well. There can be an incentive to rejoin and participate in the new ministry because of what they had invested in both the ministry and personal relationships prior to their departure.

The process of forming OPF was a long, tough development. Along the way, one of the elders left because he was discouraged by how poorly a major conflict issue was handled. The departing elder was justifiably disappointed by this circumstance and he took his family to a healthier church environment.

About a year after OPF formed, the elder who left asked if he and his family could return. The former elder was aware of the conflict resolution the elders went through to settle things. The "restoration" of relationship between him and the three elders was based on what we had learned. An awareness of our respective, personal failings allowed us to humble ourselves to one another and heal the relationships. The former elder later joined the current elder board to participate in leadership again.

Based on conversations the author has had with ministry leaders, there is an element of frustration among the younger generation of minority-race leaders over multiracial ministry. They tend to favor and value multiracial ministry more than the older generation. Through religious instruction, ethnic-specific churches can "provide a bonding among people, and they also provide a social context in which these same traditions and values can be transferred to others."[12] Hence, an older generation of racial minorities may view the church as a purveyor of ethnic cultural values to the younger generation. A multiracial church environment can pose a threat to this intention. According to Pastor YQ, this was a concern of the Korean congregation at Trinity Church that contributed to some of their difficulties.

This perceived threat should not be underestimated. During the formation of OPF, the founding leadership had exploratory conversations with leaders from two other racial minority churches[13] to consider having them be part of the creation of OPF.[14] While the younger generations highly regarded the idea, the older generations put further discussions to rest.

12. Fong, *Racial Equality*, 152.
13. One church was Asian and the other East Indian.
14. That we were willing to consider three to four churches coming together to form a new church was very optimistic and seems rather foolish given what we have learned.

Opportunities of This Ministry Approach

Feedback from the leaders indicated that change the churches would have undergone was far more than the older generation was willing to attempt.

Even though Trinity failed to stay together, and two other churches that we spoke with suffered subsequent upheaval because of generational differences, the nature of relational reconciliation can help bridge the generational gaps. Examples of how these relationships can be restored:

- A church willing to engage in tough conversations in a sensitive manner, which intercultural relationships require, has the opportunity to impact a disaffected younger generation and tired older generation.
- Resolving differences with people we do not know and fear offending can remind us of how to take care of the relationships we have taken for granted. Both younger and older generations may have dismissed or demonized the other to the point of caricature. Change and transition offers these two groups opportunities to listen and be heard.
- A fresh voice entering into the conversation may create avenues of interaction that were not previously accessible.

Again, considering the contribution the culture of Christ can make to society, Angrosino mentions that the church can "bring individuals into meaningful relationships with others in a group. Churches are among the few institutions in the United States that regularly bring immigrants, social isolates, minorities, and even socially maladjusted people into contact with the 'mainstream.'"[15] The church offers meaningful instruction about interpersonal relationships.

---

15. Angrosino, *Talking*, 48.

8

Conclusion

THE IDEA OF BRINGING two congregations together to form a multiracial church seems like it has all the makings for disaster because it means extensive change for the culture of two organizations. Yet, as a ministry approach it has merit, theologically and practically.

From a biblical perspective, a multiracial church formed from two or more congregations is a worthy and well-supported concept. The heart of God concerning grace, unity and reconciliation is unmistakable. Taking on a ministry like this requires God's call and blessing.

Practically speaking, demographic change in the U.S. means that establishing a church this way should get prayerful consideration. The benefits of this ministry are worth the difficult work required to build these congregations. The ingredients for a good start are clear vision, deliberate and courageous leadership, exhaustive communication, and a desire for and expectation of change.

Congregants will face changes that will involve altering habits and preferences that have been inculcated through racially influenced life experiences. To create an environment of intercultural respect, members will need humility and a teachable spirit.

The decision to address change and conflict management was based on observation that it was something both multiracial ministries and church mergers would have in common. It was an appropriate choice because the surveys, interviews and two written pieces on merging congregations to form a multiracial church revealed that a good deal of success or failure hinged on church leadership managing change and resolving conflict well.

Conclusion

Communication is essential for handling change and conflict. For church leadership, communicating with God's people is part of their responsibility of oversight and shepherding.

Are there churches that have "successfully" accomplished integration between single-race congregations? That would depend on one's definition of success. The three remaining Portland congregations are primarily comprised of two races—Black & Anglo, and Asian & Anglo. Will they have a multiracial congregation two to three years from now? Will they go beyond two racial groups?

Of the churches discussed in this work,[1] there were a total of nine churches that attempted to establish a multiracial congregation through merging. Two merged but no longer exist. One failed to complete the task.[2] Two, while multiracial, have less than 10 percent of the original congregants from one of the parent churches.[3] One did not fully integrate and is struggling with identity and integration.[4] The health of one church is unknown. Two have hit the five-year mark that has been described as the indicator of success or failure but their diversity ratio is unknown.[5]

The odds of success for merging congregations to create a multiracial ministry appear grim. It seems that it is hardly a pathway for ministry success. However, it is this author's contention that it is these very figures that justify the need for this book. The experiences, good and bad, described are the very things that ministries considering this type of change need to

---

1. There were two other multiracial congregations that formed through merging in Seattle that did not participate in this study. One does not exist anymore—the ministry operated between 2002 and 2004. The other congregation (a Filipino church joined an Anglo church) did not respond to requests to participate in this study. Initial contact was made but inquiries for interviews with key ministry leaders were not returned and congregants did not participate in the survey.

2. As noted earlier, Priest & Priest report that the two congregations they studied decided not to come together.

3. From Yanagihara, "A Process," 23. Yanagihara notes, "Ten years later there are no more than twenty in worship left from the former Hope Church." At best, twenty out of sixty-five remain. At worst, it is twenty out of 180. The discrepancy comes from how membership is determined—it is either by worship service attendance or names on the member roll. Laribee suggests that when a significant portion of a parent congregations has left, the church merge would not be considered successful because integration did not take place (ibid., 93).

4. Yanagihara, "A Process," 19.

5. Laribee states "Because it generally takes five years to synthesize two organizational cultures into one, 'congregational merger success' is defined here as any merger in which the merger accomplishes its desired objective in approximately five years." "Factors," 74.

hear.[6] The issues leading to "failure" are solvable but they have to be identified, and avenues to minimize impact and/or lead to resolution are needed. Hopefully, what has been presented initiates further discussion to help churches attempting this ministry approach succeed.

Furthermore, a cursory internet search reveals that a number of churches are attempting to create multiracial churches through merging. We will continue to see and hear about churches attempting this as the demographics change. Motives for reshaping their ministry include survival, preserving the legacy of their ministry, revitalizing the congregation and/or desiring to bless a younger generation.

Multi-site churches are moving in this direction. Multi-site ministries that are already multiracial have a head start in transitioning a single race congregation. Regardless of what one thinks about the "franchising" ministries, it is commendable that multi-site ministries are attempting to get the work done.

Ministries hoping to proactively engage their local community, driven by their vision and mission, should give thought to this approach for the reasons already discussed. Any ministry attempting this work models for the local community God's heart and approach toward resolving differences. Engaging race issues in a public community setting offers a unique opportunity to share the Gospel by indirect proclamation—"We are able to work through and resolve our differences across racial divides because of Jesus Christ."

The difficulties churches have encountered point to the fact that the only way a church will survive is by God's Grace. The hardships and failures reveal the limitations of humanity and the need for God to sustain these ministries. This does not suggest that those who experienced hardship and "failure" were working apart from God. Even as two sides are ardently pursuing what God has set on their hearts, things may still go sideways.[7] Fruit can continue to be borne even after the breaking of relationship.[8]

There are a number of reasons why this work can fail. If it succeeds, it is all the more apparent that God has brought about the outcome, and we are blessed when he allows us to be participants in his work.

---

6. Priest & Priest argue that these types of churches are laboratories. What goes on in these venues provides a body of information vital to improving the experiences of others.

7. In Acts 15:39, Paul and Barnabas had a strong disagreement, yet it does not mean they were disagreeable or in sin for having their row. Afterwards, the brethren do not appear to take sides but bless and send them on their way.

8. Acts 15:40–41.

Bringing congregations together to form a multiracial church deserves serious consideration because:

- There is a growing interest and need for multiracial ministry.
- It advances the kingdom by leveraging the opportunities found with an aging population and a growing racial minority population.
- It personifies the redemptive message of the gospel—God's reconciliation to mankind and reconciliation between peoples.

Personal Reflection

That God needs to be in the midst of the work is readily evident for OPF. There were a number of things I bungled as a leader, and these failings should have brought the process to a halt. I am a little surprised that it did not kill or maim the church. In spite of poor communication, muddled vision and getting off track, things came together.

The congregation I have the privilege of leading showed me enormous measures of love and grace as I struggled to head in the direction I believed God was taking us. I am humbled by their willingness to follow and stand with me through the course of the journey.

I can only imagine how much further we would be if I had followed the advice I discovered during my research. Perhaps my ignorance is our ministry's bliss. Had I known so many resources were available, I also might have been dissuaded from the attempt because of the work involved and negative outcomes, even in spite of God's call.

Other key points I learned include:

- There is no such thing as over-communication when it comes to leading God's people. People want to know what is going on—specifics are helpful, whereas uncertainty is not.
- When people express concerns about what is going on it is not a personal attack.
- Questions are good because they can reveal a weakness in communicating the vision or a hole in the plan.
- More people like the idea of multiracial churches than those who are willing to participate in it.
- Seek out people who can coach you through the various steps and aspects of ministry, especially those that will be encountered in trying

to bring congregations together (communication, conflict resolution, change management, reconciliation, multiracial/multiethnic ministry).

- Because racial and ethnic backgrounds inform how one expresses their heart-felt devotion to God, these preferences have the potential to become ingrained practices. Changing these rituals can be upsetting and will invite conflict when the "boundary" has been crossed. An individual may interpret attempts to alter their preferred practices as personal attacks and/or an affront to God.

- This book reflects part of many conversations taking place about how the church in the U.S. is doing ministry, especially across racial boundaries. Opinions about the demise of evangelicalism as it is being practiced reflect a broader concern that something needs to change.[9] Merging congregations together forces the churches involved to change their understanding of what ministry is and what works "best" to get ministry done.

Having experienced what we did in our church and the fruit of the ministry makes me thankful for the process. Creating a multiracial church by merging single-race congregations together is a feasible, valuable endeavor. Most importantly, it advances God's kingdom at a variety of levels. To start this process and see it through to its end requires keeping one's eyes on the Prize.

---

9. Spencer, "Collapse," lines 1–3.

Bibliography

Anderson, David A. *Multicultural Ministry*. Grand Rapids: Zondervan, 2004.
Anderson, Leith. *Dying for Change*. Minneapolis: Bethany House, 1990.
Angrosino, Michael V. *Talking about Cultural Diversity in Your Church: Gifts and Challenges*. Walnut Creek, CA: AltaMira, 2001.
Arsenault, Jane. *Forging Nonprofit Alliances*. San Francisco: Jossey-Bass, 1998.
Baker, Ken. "Your Church and Intercultural Ministry—Presentation Notes." In *Intercultural Ministry Manual*, by Culture ConneXions, 1–10. Charlotte: Culture ConneXions, 2007.
Baker, Ken. "Your Church and Intercultural Ministry." In *Intercultural Ministry Manual*, by Culture ConneXions, 3. Charlotte: Culture ConneXions, 2007.
Banks, Adelle. "Study: 1 Percent of Congregations Close Doors Each Year." No pages. Online: http://www.ethicsdaily.com/article_detail.cfm?AID=10577.
Barna, George. *Revolution*. Wheaton: Tyndale House, 2005.
Barrett, Devlin. "Holder: US a Nation of Cowards on Racial Matters." No pages. Online: http://news.yahoo.com/s/ap/20090218/ap_on_go_ca_st_pe/holder_race.
Bird, Warren. "Forum for Intentional Multiple Merger Churches." *Meeting Notes*. Dallas, TX: Leadership Network, November 12, 2008.
Black, Alan W. "A Marriage Model of Church Mergers." *Sociological Analysis* 49.4 (1988) 281–92.
Blake, John. "Why Many Americans Prefer Their Sundays Segregated." No pages. Online: http://www.cnn.com/2008/LIVING/wayoflife/08/04/segregated.sundays/.
Brenner, Harvey M. "Merging Congregations." FTA Thesis, Ridgefield: National Association of Temple Administrators, 2008.
Bridges, William. *Managing Transitions*. Cambridge: Perseus, 2003.
Chadwick, William. *Stealing Sheep: The Church's Hidden Problems with Transfer Growth*. Downers Grove, IL: InterVarsity, 2001.
Cho, Eugene. "Quest + Interbay = One Church." No pages. Online: http://eugenecho.wordpress.com/2007/05/07/an-amazing-story-part-2/.
———. "Quest and Its Relationship with the Evangelical Covenant Church." Edited by Fuller Theological Seminary. Fall 2008. No pages. Online: http://documents.fuller.edu/news/pubs/tnn/2008_Fall/6_quest.asp.
Christerson, Brad et al. *Against All Odds*. New York: New York University Press, 2005.
Collins, Jim. *Good to Great*. New York: HarperCollins, 2001.
———. *Good to Great and the Social Sectors*. New York: HarperCollins, 2005.
Conde-Frazier, Elizabeth et al. *A Many Colored Kingdom*. Grand Rapids: Baker Academic, 2004.

Bibliography

Crouch, Andy. *Culture Making: Recovering Our Creative Calling.* Downers Grove, IL: InterVarsity, 2008.
CTSP. "Syrian Antioch." No pages. Online: http://www.ctsp.co.il/LBS%20pages/LBS_syrian_antioch.htm.
Davis, Ken. "Multicultural Church Planting Models." *The Journal of Ministry & Theology* 7.1 (2003) 114–27.
Dealy, David M. *Change or Die.* Westport, CT: Praeger, 2006.
DeYmaz, Mark. *Building a Healthy Multi-ethnic Church.* San Francisco: Jossey-Bass, 2007.
———. "Expediting the Vision via Church Mergers." No pages. Online: http://markdeymaz.com/2008/09/merging-churche.html.
DeYoung, Curtiss Paul et al. *United by Faith.* New York: Oxford University Press, 2003.
Edwards, Korie L. *The Elusive Dream: The Power of Race in Interracial Churches.* New York: Oxford University Press, 2008.
Elmer, Duane. *Cross-Cultural Conflict.* Downers Grove, IL: InterVarsity, 1993.
Emerson, Michael O., and Christian Smith. *Divided by Faith.* New York: Oxford University Press, 2000.
Emerson, Michael O., and Rodney M. Woo. *People of the Dream.* Princeton: Princeton University Press, 2006.
Evangelical Lutheran Church in America. "Race, Ethnicity, and Culture—Freed in Christ: Race, Ethnicity and Culture." *Evangelical Lutheran Church in America.* No pages. Online: http://www.elca.org/What-We-Believe/Social-Issues/Social-Statements/Race-Ethnicity-Culture.aspx.
Ferguson, Dave. "The Multi-Site Church." No pages. Online: http://www.buildingchurchleaders.com/articles/2003/le-2003-002-21.81.html.
Fiddes, Paul S. *Participating in God: A Pastoral Doctrine of the Trinity.* Louisville, KY: Westminster John Knox, 2000.
Foland, Terry E. "Merger as a New Beginning." In *Ending with Hope: A Resource for Closing Congregations*, by Beth Ann Gaede, 64–76. Bethesda, MD: Alban Institute, 2002.
Fong, Bruce W. *Racial Equality in the Church: A Critique of the Homogeneous Unit Principle in Light of a Practical Theology Perspective.* Lanham, MD: University Press of America, 1996.
Garces-Foley, Kathleen. *Crossing the Ethnic Divide: The Multiethnic Church on a Mission.* New York: Oxford University Press, 2007.
Gladwell, Malcolm. *Outliers.* New York: Little, Brown and Company, 2008.
Gregg, Carol M. *Merging Successfully.* Bethesda, MD: The Alban Institute, 1996.
Hadaway, C. Kirk. *FACTs on Growth.* FACT2005 Survey. Hartford, CT: Hartford Institute for Religion Research, 2006.
Harris, Philip R., and Robert T. Moran. *Managing Cultural Differences.* 3rd ed. Houston: Gulf, 1991.
Hauerwas, Stanley, and Jean Vanier. *Living Gently in a Violent World: The Prophetic Witness of Weakness.* Downers Grove, IL: InterVarsity, 2008.
Hesselgrave, David J. *Planting Churches Cross-Culturally.* Grand Rapids: Baker, 2001.
Iwasaki, John. "Quest Church Makes Race a Matter of Faith." No pages. Online: http://seattlepi.nwsource.com/local/234498_faithrace29.html?dpfrom=thead.
Jones, Ezra Earl. *Strategies for New Churches.* New York: Harper & Row, 1976.
Kinoshita, Glen. "On Earth as It Is In Heaven." *Prism* (Sept/Oct 2006) 8–13, 37–38.
Koe, Richard. "Races, Generations Join in Church Merger." No pages. Online: http://www.cnnw.com/articles/articles05-00.html.

Bibliography

Kotter, John P. *Leading Change*. Boston: Harvard Business School, 1996.
Laribee, Richard A. "Factors Contributing to Success or Failure of Congregational Mergers." DMin diss., Fuller Theological Seminary, 1998.
Law, Eric H. F. *The Wolf Shall Dwell with the Lamb*. Danvers, MA: Chalice, 1993.
Long, Bill. "Periochoresis (Circumincession)." No pages. Online: http://www.drbilllong.com/Prefixes/Perichoresis.html.
Luo, Michael. "For Asian-American Churches, Integration Proves Complicated." No pages. Online: http://www.imdiversity.com/Article_Detail.asp?Article_ID=8972.
Malphurs, Aubrey. *Planting Growing Churches for the 21st Century*. Grand Rapids: Baker, 2004.
Marti, Gerardo. *A Mosaic of Believers*. Bloomington, IN: Indiana University Press, 2005.
McClendon, Kelly D. "A Map through the Minefield: Church Merger as a Strategy for Starting New Faith Communities." DMin diss., Asbury Theological Seminary, 2000.
McGavran, Donald. *Understanding Church Growth*. 2nd ed. Grand Rapids: Eerdmans, 1980.
Metzger, Paul Louis. *Consuming Jesus: Beyond Race and Class Divisions in a Consumer Church*. Grand Rapids: Eerdmans, 2007.
Murray, Stuart. *Church Planting: Laying Foundations*. Carlisle, UK: Paternoster, 1998.
Nelson, Alan. "Mega, Schmega." *Rev!*. (Mar/Apr 2008) 64–68.
Nelson, Alan, and Gene Appel. *How to Change Your Church (Without Killing It)*. Nashville, TN: Word, 2000.
Ohlemacher, Stephen. "White Americans No Longer a Majority by 2042." No pages. Online: http://abcnews.go.com/Politics/wireStory?id=5577489.
Olson, David T. *The American Church in Crisis*. Grand Rapids: Zondervan, 2008.
Ortiz, Manuel. *One New People*. Downers Grove, IL: InterVarsity, 1996.
Postman, Neil. *The End of Education: Redefining the Value of School*. New York: Knopp, 1995.
Priest, Kerstyn Bayt, and Robert J. Priest. "Divergent Worship Practices in the Sunday Morning Hour: Analysis of an 'Interracial' Church Merger Attempt." In *This Side of Heaven: Race, Ethnicity, and Christian Faith*, by Robert J. Priest and Alvaro L. Nieves, 275–91. New York: Oxford University Press, 2007.
QC. "Faith & Race." No pages. Online: http://www.seattlequest.org/content/faith-race.
Quinn, Christopher. "2 Midtown Presbyterian Churches to Merge." No pages. Online: http://www.ajc.com/search/content/metro/stories/2008/11/19/2churches.html.
Riegel, Rich. "New Life-Eastminster: Wave of Future?" March 2005. No pages. Online: http://www.midcountymemo.com/mar05_index.html.
Roberts, Chris. "Reconciliation at Unity Baptist Church." No pages. Online: http://news.minnesota.publicradio.org/features/199804/22_robertsc_unity/?refid=0.
Roberts, Sam. "Minorities Often a Majority of the Population Under 20." No pages. Online: http://www.nytimes.com/2008/08/07/us/07census.html?_r=1&sq=Minorities%20Often%20a%20Majority%20of%20the%20Population%20Under%2020&st=cse&adxnnl=1&oref=slogin&scp=1&adxnnlx=1225588240-YUU4ub451l169XC7YxS6ng.
Sande, Kenneth. *The Peacemaker*. Grand Rapids: Baker, 1997.
Schaller, Lyle E. *Reflections of a Contrarian: Second Thoughts on the Parish Ministry*. Nashville: Abingdon, 1989.
Simmons, Kim. "How to Merge Split Churches: A Case Study." DMin diss., Dallas Theological Seminary, 1996.

Bibliography

Smietana, Bob. "Southern Baptists Must Change or Die." June 1, 2008. No pages. Online: http:// thetennessean.com.
Spacek, Steve D. *Managing a Merger: A Handbook for Church Mergers*. Schwenksville, PA: Help Ministries, 1996.
Spencer, Michael. "The Coming Evangelical Collapse." No pages. Online: http://www.cs-monitor.com/2009/0310/p09s01-coop.html.
Stetzer, Ed. *Planting New Churches in a Postmodern Age*. Nashville, TN: Broadman & Holman, 2003.
Tanneberg, Ward. "An Old Church in an Aging Society." March 31, 2008. No pages. Online: http://blog.christianitytoday.com/buildingadultministries/2008/03/an_old_church_in_an_aging_soci.html.
Tomberlin, Jim. *Churches Embrace Mergers through Multisite Movement*. No pages. Online: http://www.churchsolutionsmag.com/articles/churches-embrace-mergers-through-multisite.html#.
U.S. Census Bureau. "Detailed table of race data for Washington County, Oregon." No pages. Online: http://factfinder.census.gov/servlet/DTTable?_bm=y&-context=dt&-ds_name=PEP_2007_EST&-CONTEXT=dt&-mt_name=PEP_2007_EST_G2007_T003_2007&-mt_name=PEP_2007_EST_G2007_T004_2007&-mt_name=PEP_2007_EST_G2007_T005_2007&-tree_id=807&-redoLog=false&-all_geo_types=N.
Van Engen, Chuck. "Is the Church for Everyone? Planting Multi-ethnic Congregations in North America." *Global Missiology*. October 2004. No pages. Online: http://globalmissiology.org/cms/index.php?option=com_docman&task=doc_download&gid=51&Itemid=2.
Visser t'Hooft, Willem A. *The Ecumenical Movement and the Racial Problem*. Paris: UNESCO, 1952.
Volf, Miroslav. *Exclusion and Embrace: A Theological Exploration of Identity, Otherness, and Reconciliation*. Nashville, TN: Abingdon, 1996.
Wagner, C. Peter. *Church Growth and the Whole Gospel*. San Francisco: Harper & Row, 1981.
———. *Church Planting for a Greater Harvest*. Ventura, CA: Regal, 1990.
wiktionary. *Blended Family*. No pages. Online: http://en.wiktionary.org/wiki/blended_family.
Winer, Michael, and Karen Ray. *Collaboration Handbook: Creating, Sustaining, and Enjoying the Journey*. Saint Paul, MN: Amherst H. Wilder Foundation, 1994.
Woodley, Randy. *Living in Color: Embracing God's Passion for Ethnic Diversity*. Downers Grove, IL: InterVarsity, 2001.
Yanagihara, Mariko. *And the Two Shall Become One: A Resource on Church Mergers*. Louisville, KY: Presbyterian Church (U.S.A.), 2008.
———. "A Process for Church Mergers: Asian American Churches and White Churches Becoming a New Creation in Christ." DMin diss., McCormick Theological Seminary, 2006.
Yancey, George. *One Body, One Spirit: Principles of Successful Multiracial Churches*. Downers Grove, IL: InterVarsity, 2003.
Zoll, Rachel. "More Americans Say They Have No Religion." March 9, 2009. No pages. Online: http://hosted.ap.org/dynamic/stories/R/REL_RELIGIOUS_AMERICA?SITE=VASTR&SECTION=HOME&TEMPLATE=DEFAULT.

Scripture Index

Old Testament

Leviticus
22:17–25	69n2

Isaiah
55:8–9	70

Malachi
1:8–14	69

New Testament

Matthew
6:10	13n15
6:21–26	100
18	15
18:15–22	100n62

Luke
14:26–28	69
19	12

John
12:3–5	69
12:24	98
13:35	16
13:34–35	35
17	ix, 18
17:21	12

Acts
5	82
6	16
13:1	11
15	11, 16, 16n28
15:36–39	15n25, 122n7
15:40–41	122

Romans
14	34
15	34

1 Corinthians
1:18–21	74
12	71, 82

2 Corinthians
5	71, 80
5:18	71

Galatians
2:11–14	15

Scripture Index

Ephesians
2	11
2:15–16	11
4:7–16	72n10

Philippians
4	15

Hebrews
13:17	16, 83

Revelation
5:9–14	2
7:9	13, 96
7:9–12	2

Author Index

Anderson, David A., 42, 82, 84
Anderson, Leith, 116
Angrosino, Michael V., 6, 76, 77, 119
Baker, Ken, 7
Bridges, William, 32, 97
Christerson, Brad, 5, 83, 84, 89, 99
Collins, Jim, 33
Crouch, Andy, 79
DeYmaz, Mark, 23, 24, 42, 45, 87, 94, 95
DeYoung, Curtiss Paul, 60n12, 76, 86
Edwards, Korie L., 87, 88, 95
Elmer, Duane, 72
Emerson, Michael O., 3, 9, 12, 21, 22, 82, 83, 86, 89, 91, 99, 101–3, 107n79
Foland, Terry E., 17, 40n80, 93, 96, 103, 110
Fong, Bruce W., 5, 11, 13n17, 76, 95, 118
Garces-Foley, Kathleen, 13, 28–32, 60n12, 71, 84, 97
Gregg, Carol M., 40, 97n55, 101n64
Hesselgrave, David J., 15
Jones, Ezra Earl, 101
Kotter, John P., 34
Laribee, Richard A., 9, 18, 36–40, 93, 97, 101, 109, 121n3, 121n5
Law, Eric H.F., 54
Malphurs, Aubrey, 105

Marti, Gerardo, 3, 7, 25–28, 54, 78–79, 82
McClendon, Kelly D., 40, 97, 101, 103, 109, 111
McGavran, Donald, 5, 12
Metzger, Paul Louis, 116–17
Murray, Stuart, 105
Olson, David T., 17
Ortiz, Manuel, 32
Priest, Kerstyn Bayt & Robert J., 40n76, 81, 89–92, 121n2, 122n6
Sande, Kenneth, 15n27, 59, 100
Schaller, Lyle E., 80, 81, 106, 109
Simmons, Kim, 17, 36, 36n64, 38, 93–94
Smith, Christian, 3, 7
Stetzer, Ed, 14
Van Engen, Chuck, 70, 92
Visser t'Hooft, Willem A., 73, 114
Volf, Miroslav, 12, 71, 73, 76, 85
Wagner, C. Peter, 105, 114
Woo, Rodney M., 12, 21, 22, 60n12, 92
Woodley, Randy, 85
Yanagihara, Mariko, 40, 97, 101n64, 121n3
Yancey, George, 7, 19–21, 24, 60n12, 86, 92

Subject Index

accommodation, 87
appreciation, 87, 88
assimilation, 20, 28, 85–86, 107
change management, 33, 124
church merger, 7, 9, 19, 32, 36–43, 66, 100–110, 116–17
church split, 17
communication, importance of, 62–63, 80, 91, 104, 106–7, 121, 123
conflict engagement, 5, 15
conflict management, 15, 106, 120, 124
conflict resolution, 8, 33, 36
consumerism, 116
cross cultural, 8, 23, 24, 71, 79, 84, 111
diversity, 3, 6, 7, 11–13, 22–24, 70, 71, 76, 80, 85, 92, 102, 107n79
ethnic identity, 7, 27, 28, 31, 65, 76
ethnic transcendence, 7, 28, 73, 99
ethnicity, 6, 7, 26–31, 54, 70, 73, 79, 85, 86, 92, 109
ethnocentrism, 89
Evergreen Baptist Church, 28–32
expectations, 17, 33–34, 37, 51–52, 58, 61, 81, 82, 93
factors of failure, 109
Fellowship of Faith, 42, 45, 47, 48, 55, 57, 86, 98
homogeneous church, 12, 75, 76, 78n7
heterogeneous church, 13, 75
Homogeneous Unit Principle, 5, 13–14, 27, 60, 73
humility, 59, 108, 120

intercultural, 7, 91, 107
The Journey, 42, 45–48, 51, 53–55, 57, 64, 65, 86, 93, 94, 108, 113
leadership, 11, 15–16, 17, 20–25, 29–39, 43, 49, 52–53, 55, 63–65, 91–97, 106–8, 120–21
Mosaic Church (Los Angeles, CA), 25–28
Mosaic Church (Little Rock, AR), 42
multicultural, 31, 70, 76, 79
multiethnic church, 13, 28–31, 42n88, 43, 84, 113
multiracial church, 6, 9, 11–13, 19–22, 24–25, 42, 49, 50, 60, 68, 71, 75, 76, 89–95, 106–7, 109, 118, 120, 123
multisite church, 42n88, 43
New Creation Church, 45, 47, 48, 50, 54, 58, 82
One People Fellowship, 2, 46–48, 50–52, 60, 65, 73n12, 83, 93, 96, 98, 99, 113, 118
Philadelphian Community, 45, 47, 48, 56, 60, 63, 89, 98
power, 20, 22, 23, 34, 35, 41, 54, 82, 88, 93–95
purpose, 22, 26, 60, 78n7, 97, 112
race, 6, 7, 10, 14, 27, 29, 41, 47, 51, 59, 85
racial diversity, 22
racial integration, 3, 21, 22, 87
racial reconciliation, 27, 29, 31, 60, 92, 95, 99, 112–13
racialization, 7, 32, 84
redemptive, 16, 112, 123
resource distribution, 115

Subject Index

resource dispersion, 115
single race congregation, 7, 41, 68, 94
spiritual gifts, 71, 72, 87
Trinity Church, 45–49, 58, 104, 118
trust, 16, 18, 23, 35, 57–59, 62–63, 107–8

unity, 18, 70, 73, 88, 92, 99
vision, 20, 34, 35, 53, 63–64, 96–98, 103, 107
Wilcrest Baptist Church, 12–13, 21, 24

www.ingramcontent.com/pod-product-compliance
Lightning Source LLC
Chambersburg PA
CBHW070918160426
43193CB00011B/1513